IMPERIAL STUDIES, No. 4.

General Editor :—A. P. NEWTON, M.A., D.Lit. B.Sc., F.S.A.
Rhodes Professor of Imperial History in the University of London.

BRITISH POLICY AND CANADA, 1774-1791

British Policy and Canada

1774 - 1791

A Study in 18th Century Trade Policy

BY

GERALD S. GRAHAM

M.A. Queen's University, Canada; A.M. Harvard; Ph.D. Cambridge.
Late Sir George Parkin Scholar at Trinity College, Cambridge.

WITH TWO MAPS

GREENWOOD PRESS, PUBLISHERS
WESTPORT, CONNECTICUT

Library of Congress Cataloging in Publication Data

Graham, Gerald Sandford, 1903-
British policy and Canada, 1774-1791.

Based on the author's thesis, Cambridge.
Reprint of the 1930 ed. published by Longmans, Green, London, which was issued as no. 4 of Imperial studies of the Royal Empire Society.
Bibliography: p.
1. Great Britain--Commercial policy. 2. Great Britain--Colonies--Commerce. 3. Canada--Commerce. I. Title. II. Series: Royal Commonwealth Society. Imperial studies, no 4.
HF1533.G7 1974 382'.0942'071 74-136532
ISBN 0-8371-5453-7

Originally published in 1930 for The Royal Empire Society
by Longmans, Green and Co., London

Reprinted in 1974 by Greenwood Press,
a division of Williamhouse-Regency Inc.

Library of Congress Catalog Card Number 74-136532

ISBN 0-8371-5453-7

Printed in the United States of America

FOREWORD TO THE IMPERIAL STUDIES SERIES

There are, it has been said, three British Empires; the first the Empire of early conquest and romance, the second, that which began in 1776 and developed into the great Victorian Empire, the third, that which is now arising under the new title of the British Commonwealth of Nations.

The story and the poetry of the first has been adequately treated; the last is not yet ripe for the historian. The second has hardly received the full treatment which it deserves: its problems, political, geographical, social and economic, offer a wide field for investigation; it is moreover of special urgency to spend research upon them now, while men are still alive who spoke with pioneers and proconsuls of the last century.

This is, in the main, the epoch with which this series of "Imperial Studies" monographs will deal. Strictly speaking, they appear under the ægis of the Imperial Studies Committee, which works in connection with the Royal Empire Society.

It is the belief of that Committee that important works of research are being undertaken at our Universities, old and new, and elsewhere, which ought to be published. These monographs are serious and scholarly attempts to fill in gaps in the story, political, social or economic, of our Imperial development. Some will have value both as critical studies of the past and for the light they throw upon modern problems; others will deal with natural environment or with circumstances as they exist to-day. In any case questions of commerce and economies will certainly not be neglected.

The Series has been designed and endowed not so much for writers of established reputation as for those who are mature in mind but young in years; they are, in fact, works of ripe scholarship by men and women trained in the twentieth century.

M. J. RENDALL,
Chairman of the Imperial Studies Committee.

THE ROYAL EMPIRE SOCIETY,
LONDON, W.C.2.
September, 1930.

To

FLORENCE MARIAN GRAHAM

" Nature, reason and observation all plainly point out to us our true object of national policy, which is commerce ; the inexhaustible source of wealth and power to a people."

Considerations on the Policy, Commerce and Circumstances of the Kingdom, London, 1771.

" Commerce as soon as it leaves the domestic sphere becomes really a branch of government ; what we call empire is as much the expansion of national trade, as it is the overseas settlement of British subjects."

Morison, J. L., *The Eighth Earl of Elgin.*

PREFACE

THIS book is chiefly concerned with the development of trade policy in the new British Empire after the loss of the American colonies. The first four chapters may, therefore, really be considered as introductory to the main theme—'Canada within the Navigation System.' Until 1783 Canada played no vital part in the British Trade and Navigation System. Up to that date she was a conquered French province, valued by merchant interests for her rich supplies of furs and fish, but held in some disdain by most British statesmen who, in accordance with the best mercantilist tradition, preferred acquisitions in the tropics. The successful revolution of the American colonies brought an end to this indifference. The loss to the Empire of valuable sources of supply meant that England, if she were to preserve her self-contained economic system must seek to repair the gap in the triangular trade which so closely affected her West Indian islands and threatened to weaken her naval strength. The American revolution brought about no alteration in the accepted mercantilist theories of colonial administration, but it was the means of forcing Canada into new prominence, making her for the first time an important factor in British diplomacy.

It would be well-nigh an endless task to thank all those who in various ways have contributed to the making of this book. Most of its matter was contained in a thesis accepted for the degree of Doctor of Philosophy by the University of Cambridge. I must confess my especial gratitude to Professor J. Holland Rose whose help and encouragement have followed me throughout the period of my work. I should also like to record my thanks to the founders of the Sir George Parkin

Foundation, Mrs. Buck and Miss Margaret Beith of "Noverings," Bosbury, Hereford, whose generosity in the form of scholarships perpetuates the name and spirit of a great Canadian, and to the Imperial Studies Committee of the Royal Empire Society, who have undertaken the responsibility, and, with the generous assistance of Trinity College, Cambridge, the financial burden of publication. I shall not attempt to express my debt to Cambridge, nor to explain the reality of inspiration that has come to me from two years' dwelling in her quiet courts.

G. S. G.

TRINITY COLLEGE,
CAMBRIDGE.
August, 1930.

CONTENTS

MAPS

ABBREVIATIONS EMPLOYED.

Brit. Mus.	Pamphlets or documents contained in the British Museum.
C.A.	Report of the Canadian Archivist on the Archives for the year designated.
C.O.	Colonial Office papers in the Public Record Office, followed consecutively by series number, volume number and folio number. In cases where volumes are not foliated the reference can be ascertained by means of the date.
C.H.R.	Canadian Historical Review.
E.H.R.	English Historical Review.
A.H.R.	American Historical Review.

INTRODUCTION

THE CHOICE OF A DOMINION

When Wolfe achieved his decisive victory on the Plains of Abraham, the continent of North America was almost entirely in the hands of three great powers, France, Spain and Great Britain. By the terms of the Treaty of Paris, 1763, Britain took over the whole continent east of the Mississippi, excluding the city of New Orleans. The French dominions in North America vanished with the exception of two tiny islands in the Gulf of St. Lawrence.[1]

Until *annus mirabilis* suddenly changed the territorial scheme of things, Britain's most valued possessions had been situated in tropical or semi-tropical zones, and were rated by all intelligent statesmen in proportion as they furnished commodities which the Mother Country could not herself produce or which she would otherwise have to purchase from foreign nations. The importation of these colonial raw products was confined entirely to Britain, who managed at the same time to retain a monopoly of all export. Both monopolies served a great purpose—the augmentation of British naval strength by the entire exclusion of foreign shipping.

For the greater part of the eighteenth century, this theory of colonial utility remained general throughout Europe, and formed the central arch of what was known as the mercantilist system. Its economic tenets did more than influence policy; they dictated it. The means which Britain adopted to retain the full benefits of the system did on occasion prove more liberal or more effective than those of rival states, but on the whole, the principle was the same for them all—to secure to themselves respectively, the most important of the productions of the colonies and to retain to themselves exclusively the great

[1] St. Pierre and Miquelon.

advantage of supplying those colonies with European goods and manufactures.[1]

By mercantilist standards, tropical dependencies such as the West India islands were held in far higher repute than the northern New England provinces.[2] Bryan Edwards, the great historian of the West Indies could say unblushingly that, "If the comparative merit of colonies be examined, we may safely assert that none ever existed so reconcilable with the best principles of political economy as those which the European nations possess in the West Indies,[3] . . . every article of their products and returns being in fact as truly British property, as the tin which is found in the mines of Cornwall, and their staples are the more valuable inasmuch as they differ from the commodities produced at home: for they supply the Mother Country not only with what she must otherwise purchase from foreigners for her own use, but with a superfluity besides for foreign consumption."[4] Massachusetts might provide a few masts for the Navy, but Jamaica and her neighbours built up carrying trade and sea-power, produced sugar for all England and maintained in luxury a politically powerful nabob class.

But the strength and popularity of that standard was to be tested by the victorious outcome of the Seven Years' War. The redistribution of territories following the peace presented to the negotiators a perplexing problem. It amounted, generally speaking, to a choice between a sugar island in the Caribbean and almost half the North American continent. Was the final choice of Canada, coming at a time when the Industrial Revolution was only beginning to gain momentum, brought about by a more modern understanding of the value of northern

[1] Bryan Edwards, *History, Civil and Commercial, of the British Colonies in the West Indies*, Introduction.

[2] With reference to New England, a pamphleteer in 1777 exposes the still lively prejudice against northern colonies. "They rival Britain in commerce. They carry their corn and other produce to foreign markets, where they meet the productions of Britain, and occasion them to lay on hand by underselling them. They likewise run away with the principal share of the great source of British wealth and naval power, the fishery of Newfoundland. . . . Can it be the interest of Britain to support colonies that reap every essential advantage of commerce with herself, and at the same time exempt them from all authority or allegiance but what they please to admit." *Observations*, etc., Anon., London, 1777.

[3] Bryan Edwards, *History of the West Indies*, Book V, Vol. III, p. 456.

[4] *Ibid.*, III, p. 465.

colonies,[1] or did the old mercantilist prepossession for tropical colonies continue for some time longer? In short, was the decision to retain Canada a matter of political chance rather than of conscious alteration in established policy?

It is difficult to penetrate the haze which surrounds the tangled negotiations preceding peace. That the decision was influenced by a rational balancing of northern against southern colonies in the minds of the public and of statesmen is questionable. Public opinion in the modern democratic sense hardly existed. Even in the momentous year 1792, the astute Talleyrand wrote to his Foreign Office—" The truth is that the mass of the nation is generally indifferent to all those political discussions which cause so much stir among us."[2] There was an enormous amount of pamphleteering on the relative values of the two territories;[3] but since they were of highly partisan flavour, setting forth the platforms of factions, they are of little avail in adjudging what men of affairs really thought on the question. The House of Commons alone reflected the realities of the situation, and that body, elected in the typically eighteenth-century manner, represented not the people, but a politically conscious minority, the landed aristocracy.[4]

Yet apart from men like Pitt and Shelburne, few of this ruling class knew a great deal about Canada. Voltaire voiced the opinion of the average Englishman as well as Frenchman, when he wrote of the sterile frozen lands of cannibal savages in contending for which the Government wasted more money than all Canada was worth.[5] Samuel Johnson saw in Canada only a cold, uncomfortable, uninviting region with nothing but furs and fish, inhabited by a people in perpetual regret of the native land.[6] If New England had never been a popular

[1] See Beer, G. L., *British Colonial Policy*, 1754–65, Chap. VIII, pp. 133–4.

[2] Despatch of May 23, 1792; quoted Butler, J. R. M., *Passing of the Great Reform Bill*, p. 21.

[3] See Grant, W. L., *A.H.R.*, July, 1912, p. 73, for a summary of this pamphlet war; also Lecky, *History of England*, Vol. III, Chap. XII, *passim.*

[4] See Oldfield, *History of the Boroughs*, Vol. VI, pp. 285–8. Even as late as the 90's, 87 peers between them procured the return of 218 members for England and Wales; *Parl. Papers of John Robinson*, Introd., p. ix; and Namier, L. B., *Structure of Politics at the Accession of George III*, p. 86.

[5] *Précis du Siècle de Louis XV*, Chap. XXXV, *passim; Essai sur les Moeurs*, CLI.

[6] Boswell, *Life of Johnson*

member of the self-sufficient family, it was not likely that a land of cannibals, furs and fish would evoke any greater enthusiasm. Only inspired or eccentric minds saw a future in Canada. Informed minds were few and far between.

One conclusion, therefore, stands apparent. The final explanation of the Treaty of Paris must be sought not in the conflict of opinion, but rather in the play of factions, in the wrangling and bargaining of Pelhams, Bedfords, Grenvillites, Rockinghams and King's Friends,[1] with the dark figure of mercantile interests ever in the background.

As it happened, those commercial interests most concerned with the question were, in the end, the most consequential forces in deciding it. The powerful and well organized West India planters and merchants had no immediate interest in Canada, but they were vitally interested in any settlement which affected their sugar trade. Influential business men such as Beckford, Hodges and Price, men who were at the same time London Councillors and hearty supporters of Pitt, were unanimous that the French should be totally expelled both from Canada and Newfoundland, but they opposed Pitt when he suggested the acquisition of Guadaloupe in addition.[2] Their point of view was that of all the great West India planters in London and may be summarized as follows: the acquisition of French sugar islands would injure existing British islands by reducing the price of sugar.[3] Tropical expansion would mean not only increased production and falling prices, but the gradual decline of the older communities such as Barbados and the Leeward Islands. On the other hand, the retention of Canada might offer the opportunity of an enlarged colonial market for molasses, rum and sugar.[4]

[1] Political divisions are discussed in Winstanley, D. A., *Chatham and the Whig Opposition;* Namier, L. B., *The Structure of Politics at the Accession of George III;* Trevelyan, G. O., *The Early Life of Charles James Fox,* and *The American Revolution;* for an illuminating short account see Alvord, C. W., *Mississippi Valley in British Politics,* Vol. I, Chap. I.

[2] Not until out of office in 1762 was Pitt in a position to urge the acquisition of both Guadaloupe and Canada. For information regarding Pitt's relations with the City, I am indebted to Dr. H. W. V. Temperley. See also Kate Hotblack, *Chatham's Colonial Policy,* Chap. IV, *passim.*

[3] See Mauduit, I., *Considerations on the Present German War,* 5th ed. London, 1761. In his *Development of the British West Indies* F. W. Pitman refers to the West India planters' attempt to promote a monopoly.

[4] See Kimball, G., *Correspondence of William Pitt,* Vol. II, pp. 380–2, 404. Contains references to the new openings for British manufactures in the hinterland of Canada.

The existence of such organized profiteering is well borne out by the Board of Trade. At the time of the preliminary negotiations, they reported that "the English wanted more sugar land to plant not only to supply foreign markets, but also to increase the quantity for home consumption and thereby reduce the price of a commodity now become exorbitant."[1] It is thus apparent that what the planters feared was competition. Guadaloupe as a rival would seriously interfere with an attempt to perpetuate monopoly prices in England. That they should use their power to influence the trend of the negotiations in favour of a continuance of that monopoly is not therefore astonishing. Ten years later, at a time when West India planters were cursing the fate that made them provisionally dependent on Canada for supply, Lord Sheffield was able to satirize them thus—" . . . but this Canada which is now so despised by West India planters, is the country for which the finest possessions in the West Indies were given up, through the influence of those planters, because an accession of sugar colonies would bring a greater quantity of produce to market and might lower the price and their profit."[2]

On the other hand, it has been argued by some historians that the decision of British statesmen to demand Canada was influenced in greater degree by their desire to remove the menace of French aggression from the English colonies to the south—" They took Canada, not indeed to make use of it themselves, but to prevent the French from making use of it."[3] It is impossible to estimate the influence of this view, which was undoubtedly held by Pitt and men like William Shirley.[4]

[1] Board of Trade Report, (Brit. Mus.) Add. MS., 35913, fol. 73. Strangely enough Shelburne, so rarely given to exaggeration, declared in 1762, that " Jamaica if cultivated to the height could produce more sugar than all Europe consumed." Speech of 1762, Shelburne MS. (Univ. of Michigan), vol. 165. Board of Trade reports give no justification for this speculation, although the planters may have to a degree limited the output.

[2] *Observations on the Commerce of the American States*, Introduction, p. xxxv.

[3] Wallace, W. S., " The Beginnings of British Rule in Canada," *C.H.R.*, Vol. VI, 1925.

[4] The war had been waged by Pitt and his colleagues mainly with the view of conquering Canada and ending the intolerable situation of the British seaboard colonies in North America. Pitt was still feared, though out of office, and his emphasis on the strategic value of the colony could not have been without effect. See Kimball, *Correspondence of William Pitt*, Vol. I, p. 132, and Vol. II, p. 251.

Strategic advantages may have been considered, but they were never definitely asserted by the official negotiators, Bute and Bedford.[1] In fact, the Bedfordites with Franklin's perspicacity were by no means in favour of the acquisition of Canada. They claimed that England would be weakened by too many colonies and they doubted the wisdom of removing a hostile colony from the borders of the increasingly independent Thirteen.[2] Bute wrote to Bedford in July 1761[3]: "The Duke of Bedford cannot wish for peace more sincerely than I do; but let that peace prove in some measure answerable to the conquest we have made. Can ministers answer for it to the public, if they advise the King to sit down satisfied with a barren country, not equal in value to the duchies of Lorrain and Barr, and yet an acquisition invidious from its vast extent. . . . Why not rather out of all our rich conquests, reserve to posterity something that will bring in a clear and certain revenue, to enable them to pay the interest of the enormous debt we have by this most expensive war laid upon them?" But Bedford knew that any alternative acquisition in the form of a sugar island was out of the question. Hence he opposed Pitt's plan for the conquest of Martinique, as being wasteful effort. The West India interest, he knew, would resist the permanent acquisition of that island as strongly as they had opposed the retention of Guadaloupe.[4] That the negotiators did finally sacrifice these two islands as well as St. Lucia to France seems explicable only by their intense desire for peace, but more directly by their subservience to the powerful planter class.

Nevertheless, it is inconceivable that the West India interest with all their wealth could have turned the scale, if there had been any antagonism on the part of the men of "broad acres." England was still an agricultural country, and the landed gentry still retained political predominance.[5] In the words of

[1] The best source for Bute's and Bedford's attitude during the negotiations is to be found in the *Grenville Papers*, Vol. I, *passim*, and *Bedford Correspondence*, iii, *passim*.

[2] *Bedford Correspondence*, Vol. III, p. 17; quoted by Alvord, *op. cit.*, p. 55.

[3] Bute to Bedford, London, July 12, 1761, *Bedford Correspondence*, iii, 32.

[4] Bedford to Bute, July 9, 1761, *ibid.*, iii, 25.

[5] "The merchant sandwiched in between the head of the family and the younger son, cut but a poor figure, whilst the manufacturer did not appear

Wilberforce, the country gentlemen were still the very " nerves and ligatures " of the body politic. There were a few increasingly aggressive bankers, traders and West India merchants in the House; but they received little recognition in the way of office.[1] The embryo manufacturing interests had no representation at all.[2] So long as the country interests remained mainly agricultural, the influence of the great land-owning peers was bound to be powerful. It is obvious that no important decision could possibly have been taken without their approval or passive neutrality.

Shirley and Shelburne had no part in the negotiations; but they did attempt to educate ruling class opinion in favour of the northern province. As early as October, 1745, William Shirley, when Governor of Massachusetts, had written to the Duke of Newcastle advising the reduction of all Canada.[3] He pointed out such advantages as the complete control of the fur trade, the securing of the whole cod fishery in the Gulf and River St. Lawrence and in the neighbourhood of Newfoundland; independence of all foreign states for naval stores, a market for rum and woollen manufactures, a stimulus to shipping and a nursery for seamen. With customary mercantilist altruism he concluded—" and what seems to make these advantages still the more valuable is, that they weaken the power of France whilst they add to that of Great Britain."

Lord Shelburne, that keen student of colonies, who had become a member of the Board of Trade, expressed a similar point of view in a most important speech of 1762.[4] In it, he

at all. . . . It was plain that during the greater part of the 18th century, England was content to be ruled by landlords." Veitch, G. S. *The Genesis of Parliamentary Reform*, p. 20. See also Namier, L. B., *op. cit.*, pp. 7 and 86.

[1] Veitch, *ibid.*, p. 20; Namier, *ibid.*, p. 61.

[2] Veitch, *ibid.*, p. 20.

[3] *Correspondence of William Shirley;* edited by C. H. Lincoln, pp. 284–5.

[4] Shelburne MS., vol. 165. The William L. Clements Library, Ann Arbor, Michigan. Transcripts with Stevens and Brown, 4, Trafalgar Square, London, S.W.1. This important speech is contained in a paper, undated and unclassified, and it is not printed in Hansard. There is no mention made of it, either in the *Fifth Report* of the Historical MSS. Commission, Part I, 1876, which catalogues the Collection, or in the *Reports* of the Canadian Archives for 1912 and 1921. It was obviously the speech which Shelburne made on December 9, 1762, in defence of the preliminary articles of Peace. Lord Fitzmaurice, in his *Life of Shelburne*, remarks that: " No record of his speech on this occasion is preserved." See Vol. I, p. 179 (ed. 1875), and p. 137 (ed. 1912). cf. Temperley, H. W., The Peace of Paris, Chap. XVII, of *Cambridge History of the British Empire*, vol. I, p. 504.

gave prophetic utterance to opinions which were later to form the basis of a new estimate of northern colonies. " Common sense," he declared, " dictates to us that we must restore some of our conquests to make peace tolerable to our enemies—without this we must have waged eternal war." He disparaged the Island of Guadaloupe as being a trifling object in comparison with North America. Wherever sugar grows, such was his argument, population decreases, and sugar colonies weaken and depopulate the Mother Country. The total exclusion of the French from Canada and of the Spaniards from Florida would give Great Britain the universal empire of that extended coast, would make the inhabitants easy in their possessions, open up a new field of commerce with many Indian nations, and furnish great additional resources to the increase of our naval power. By the acquisition of Canada " Britain gains the clothing of many Indian nations, besides 70,000 ' Acadians ' [French Canadians], which in so cold a climate must annually consume full £200,000 value of British manufactures; the returns for which must be made part in fish exported to foreign markets; about £60,000 value in furs and quantities of oil, whalebone and iron." He referred to the forge at St. Maurice, " which has in years past produced 400 tons of Bar and Cast Iron," and if proper encouragement is given " this country might be made to supply all the materials imported from the Baltic." It would provide good ballast for hemp and flax, for the growth of which the climate is suitable, and these three articles, being paid for in British manufactures instead of money as they are now paid for to Russia and Sweden, would be an immense gain of one half a million sterling. There were also unlimited opportunities for obtaining lumber supplies, and developing a ship-building industry, factors so essential to the welfare of the West Indies and the all-important Fisheries.[1]

The Board of Trade were more restrained, but none the less agreed. They submitted that " Guadaloupe is well worthy to be retained if possible, but not in an equal degree with North America; and if something must be given up, this island

[1] See Lords of Trade to Egremont, June 8, 1763, for a further consideration of the benefits arising from the cession. Shortt and Doughty, *Docs., relating to the Constitutional History of Canada*, Vol. I, p. 132.

seems the fittest." On the other hand, distinguishing North America under the heads of Canada, Louisiana and Newfoundland, they contended that "the Newfoundland Fishery as a means of wealth and power is of more worth than both the aforementioned provinces."[1]

The Board of Trade expressed the average English statesman's evaluation of Canada. Shelburne's plea for the northern territory as a potential market for £200,000 of English manufactures was premature. England was only approaching the verge of her industrialization. Although the woollen manufacturers had been a favoured class all through the eighteenth century, there is no evidence in this instance to show that their influence or interest in the negotiations was anything but negligible. Dreams of a new woollen market may have raised hopes in the minds of some few optimistic landowners,[2] but a nation which thought in terms of seamanship and naval supremacy continued to accept the Board of Trade's dictum, and regard the fisheries of Newfoundland and the Gulf as far more important than the province of Canada.[3]

Accordingly, it was but a grudging recognition that Canada received within the imperial economic circle. The almost casual acquisition of the colony by Bute and Bedford and the indifferent reception accorded it by Parliament, show small evidence of a more modern or more enlightened appreciation of the value of northern colonies. The decision of 1763 marked no alteration in the methods and principles which governed the workings of the old colonial system. The merchant-manufacturing interests which within two decades were to become so powerful a factor in British politics, had not yet begun to assert themselves seriously against the power of the West Indies.[4] British policy was still directed towards the creation of a self-sufficient economic empire, and tropical

[1] Board of Trade Report, 1761. (Brit. Mus.) Add. MS. 35913, fol. 73.

[2] The influence of manufacturing and landed woollen interests is, I believe, over-emphasized by G. L. Beer in his *British Colonial Policy, 1754–65*, Ch. VIII. The progress of industrialism in England and the consequent increasing importance of the manufacturer are similarly exaggerated.

[3] Referring to the French attitude towards Canada prior to the negotiations, Charles Jenkinson wrote to George Grenville, "In a word, Canada without her fisheries is in their own opinions hardly worth their acceptance, and if the Fisheries could be otherwise secured to them, they will have little occasion for the former." *Grenville Papers*, I, p. 342.

[4] See Penson, L. M., *Colonial Agents of the British West Indies*, *passim*, for references to West India strength in English politics.

colonies remained, in general opinion, the most valuable subsidiary parts.[1] Except as a strategic base for the development of sea-power through the fisheries, Canada had little direct claim on the attention of British statesmen who continued to base their estimates of colonial worth on the time-worn standards of Mercantilism.

[1] In 1764, it was proposed in Providence that the American colonies should undertake a continental agreement to suspend trade with the British West Indies, in order to strike a blow at the West India interest in Parliament. It is an interesting reflection on the conflict of interests between the two types of colonies. See Schlesinger, A. M., *Colonial Merchants and the American Revolution* (Columbia University, *Studies in History and Economics*, etc). N.Y., 1917.

CHAPTER I

THE POLITICAL SITUATION IN ENGLAND, 1763–83

"A great empire and little minds go ill together."—EDMUND BURKE.

IN the opening pages of his *Thoughts on the Causes of the Present Discontents* (1770), Burke describes with majestic fury the lamentable ineffectiveness of the Government during the period following the Peace of 1763, a description which remained relevant long after the time in which he wrote. "Nothing," he cried, "can equal the futility, the weakness, the rashness, the timidity, the perpetual contradiction in the management of our affairs. . . ." His contemporary indictment has fairly well borne the tests of later research.

From 1763 to 1772, there had been no less than twelve changes in the office of Secretary of State, and the names of Egremont, Halifax, Shelburne, Hillsborough and Conway appear and often reappear in startling succession. Between 1761 and 1768, the Presidency of the Board of Trade changed seven times,[1] and although this had little effect on the personnel of the Board, such shiftings and variations made a consistent ministerial policy out of the question. Added to this, the Board of Trade, the Secretary of State and the Privy Council, all dabbled in varying degrees with colonial affairs, with the intermittent assistance of the Treasury, the Customs and the Admiralty. "The military corresponded with the Secretary of State; civil officers sometimes with the Secretary, sometimes with the Board of Trade; the Navy with the Admiralty on matters not necessarily naval; engineers with the Ordnance Board; and officers of the Revenue with the Treasury."[2]

[1] See Basye, A. H., *The Board of Trade*, p. 146. Also an article by the same author—"The Secretary of State for the Colonies, 1768–82," *A.H.R.*, Vol. 28, 1922.

[2] Thomas Pownall, *Administration of Colonies* (London, 1768), pp. 12–14, 18. Pownall makes a strong plea for centralized control. "That part of the government which should administer this great and important branch of

"My long experience in colony affairs and thorough knowledge of their state," declared Under-Secretary William Knox, with a complacency which in his case was perhaps warranted, "has shown me that the great source of all our disputes and difficulties lay in the mutability of the measures of Government, from the want of system and their partaking of the fashion of the times and wearing the complications of their several authors."[1]

History and philosophy have never counted for much in politics, and during that corrupt period of party flux, clear-thinking statescraft was never valued less, or gold and trade more. Outside a narrow circle which included men such as Chatham, Burke, Shelburne, Pownall or Knox, there was little understanding of colonial conditions, and even less opportunity of consistently applying what knowledge there existed. The kaleidoscope of groups and parties made a continuous studied policy practically impossible until the advent of the North Ministry in 1770, with the triumph of the King. Only then did the formation of a strong Coalition, along with the creation of an American department and the appointment of a permanent Under-Secretary seem to indicate at last a certain unity of command in the conduct of overseas affairs.[2]

That balanced collection of mediocrities, the North Ministry, did possess certain unity of heart as well as incapacity. They not only survived, but actually grew in strength with time and kingly favour until they became almost impregnable to parliamentary attack in either House. George III, with his army of

business, ought, in the first place, to be the centre of all information and application from all the interests and powers which form it, to be able fully, uniformly and efficiently to distribute its directions and orders. . . . In the first place there never was yet any one department formed for this purpose; and in the next, if there was, let any one acquainted with the business dare to say, how any attempt of such a department would operate on the jealousies of the others. Whenever, therefore, it is thought proper (as most certainly it will, some time or other, tho' perhaps too late) to form such a department, it must be sovereign and supreme, as to everything relating to it; or to speak plainly out, MUST BE A SECRETARY OF STATE'S OFFICE IN ITSELF," p. 12.

[1] *Extra-Official State Papers*, Part I, Appendix V, p. 14.

[2] John Yorke wrote to the Earl of Hardwicke in July of that year: "As to America I do not believe all the long wigs you enumerate will be able to fall upon any right and yet popular system for quieting that country. The only chance would be a well-united and well approved ad[ministratio]n at home, and the wisdom of this reign has been to make that as difficult as possible." (Brit. Mus.) Add. MS. 35375, fol. 63.

nearly 200 placemen in the House of Commons,[1] held the reins with firmness and understanding; and in North he possessed an ideal type of overseer.

The Opposition handled things badly. Split up into varied groups of competing interests, their only tie of any strength was opposition to the personal rule of the King. The Chatham Whigs, disbelieving in party government and deriving their main support from commercial middle-class London, gradually dwindled away. From them drifted the reputable Grenvillites; and the disreputable Bedfordites had long ago become assimilated by the King's Friends at a "price per lot." The largest fragment of the Opposition was the Rockingham Whigs, of whom Burke was the intellectual guide. Their strength came from two sources—chiefly from the great landowners in the House of Lords, which then numbered less than 200 Members,[2] and in part from the merchants whose trade was in danger and who were opposed to any drastic methods likely to effect a breach with their American customers. But this substantial fragment was also doomed to disintegrate. Many Nonconformist Whigs had continued to show a real sympathy with the American cause, and not a few had agreed with David Hume, that "if the Court carried the day in America, the English constitution would infallibly perish." With Independence proclaimed as an objective, the main body threw their weight in favour of an out and out recognition. Chatham and Shelburne were left stranded almost alone, with Camden and Richmond wavering.[3] This was in January, 1778, and in the next month the House of Bourbon recognized the Independence of the United States of America and changed the struggle from a civil war to a fight for life.

The question of Independence revealed one common motive amid the welter of party strife, and serves to express again the influence of mercantilist theory in the determination of colonial policy. Cutting across old lines of personality, privilege and self-seeking, one broad principle of action remained to

[1] *Annual Register*, Vol. xiii, Historical, p. 72.
[2] Newman, B., *Life of Burke*, p. 36.
[3] See Temperley, H. W. V., "Chatham, North and America," *Quarterly Review*, Oct., 1914.

link men together regardless of party politics—the principle of colonial subordination and commercial utility.

Even men with imagination, such as Chatham or Pownall, although they were opposed to offensive taxation, refused to contemplate any alteration in a commercial policy which aimed at making the colonies profitable to England. The triple monopoly of import, export and carriage was reconcilable only with an absolute dependence and a complete central control. Hence, in the Britain of that day, there could be no mediating theory of compromise. Imperial theory, if such it could be called, was limited for all general purposes to the choice between absolute independence and absolute subordination.

That broad imperialist who loved the colonies " as men prizing and setting a just value upon that inestimable blessing, liberty," men too great " to be embraced save in the arms of affection " would not permit them to manufacture a single hoof nail. Pitt further declared—" If I could persuade myself that they entertain the most distant intention of throwing off the legislative supremacy and great constitutional superintending power and control of the British legislature, I should myself be the first person . . . to enforce that power by every exertion this country is capable of making."[1] " I will as soon subscribe to transubstantiation as to sovereignty by Right for the Colonies."[2] Thomas Pownall was equally firm. The Mother Country, he declared, had an exclusive right to the external profits of colonial labour and custom. " As it is the right, so it becomes the duty of the Mother Country to cultivate, to protect and govern the colonies : which nurture and government should precisely direct its care to two essential points, first, that all the profits of the produce and manufactures of these colonies centre finally in the Mother Country : and secondly, that the colonies continue to be the sole and proper customers of the Mother Country. To these two points, collateral with the interests, rights and welfare of the colonies, every measure of administration, every law of trade should tend."[3]

[1] Thackeray, Francis, *Life of Chatham*, Vol. II, p. 279.

[2] Temperley, *op. cit.*

[3] *The Administration of the Colonies*, 4th edition, 1768, p. 40. The British Museum copy of this edition contains annotations from the hand of Edmund

But at the other extreme, on the side for separation and independence, was a tiny minority, known as the "œconomists."[1] They were a generation ahead of their time in so far as they proclaimed the futility of trade laws in contributing to the profit of England. Hence they were a minority. Yet, these ancestors of *laissez-faire*, these early "Little Englanders"—Tucker, Priestley, Hume, Townshend and Arthur Young—made the first assaults on the Chinese Wall of Mercantilism. "Common sense," said Josiah Tucker, in the early stages of the revolution, "might have informed us that Trade depends on Interest alone and on no other connection or obligation. The fact is that the colonies never did trade with the Mother Country with an interest merely to serve us, and not themselves. . . . Mutual Interest was the only tie between America and Great Britain at all times and seasons, and this Principle will hold good, I will be bold to say, till the end of time, whether they are dependent or independent of us."[2] There is irony in his reference to the fruits of 1763. "Canada, when it has grown rich by our means and our Capitals, will assuredly set up for Independence as you have done, and in a few years we shall have the same scenes of Malevolence and Ingratitude displayed there. . . ."[3] "He who would free France from her colonies would be her true friend," said Arthur Young,[4] and later, on the eve of the French Revolution, he decried transmarine dominions as sources of weakness, to renounce which would be wisdom.[5] David Hume might well have explained much international rivalry to-day, when he drew attention to the general belief that one nation's commercial progress must inevitably be at the expense of another. "In opposition to this narrow and malignant opinion, I will venture to assert that the increase of riches and commerce in

Burke. On the margin he remarks, in this instance, satirically, "The author must know that all our plantation laws have those two points constantly in their view and that nothing is less necessary than general information on this subject."

[1] A name applied by Henry Brougham in his *Inquiry into the Colonial Policy of European Powers*.

[2] *Four Letters*, Vol. I, p. 9, 1774; republished 1783.

[3] Tracts, No. V, *The respective Pleas and Arguments of the Mother Country distinctly set forth*. London, 1775.

[4] Quoted by Wilhelm Roscher, *Kolonien*, etc., p. 227.

[5] Arthur Young, *Travels in France*, p. 262.

any one nation, instead of hurting, commonly promote the riches and commerce of all its neighbours."[1]

Adam Smith did not belong to the school of *laissez-faire*. He was not a Little Englander, for he rejected the alternative of separation on the grounds of national sentiment. But he was by far the bitterest and ablest opponent of monopoly. If he did see the political advantages in the Navigation Acts, he was equally convinced that they by no means compensated for the disadvantages. "If the colony trade is advantageous for Great Britain," he declared, "it is not by means of the monopoly, but in spite of the monopoly."[2] On the eve of the Declaration of Independence, he attempted to show that the gains from the system were illusory, that England had gained nothing either in military strength or in revenue from the possession of colonies, but on the contrary had suffered loss and accumulated debt.

Yet Smith himself realized that his was a voice crying in the wilderness. The influence of private interests was too great. "To attempt to reduce the army," he remarked somewhat bitterly, "would be as dangerous, as it has now become, to attempt to diminish in any respect the monopoly which our manufacturers have obtained against us. This monopoly has so much increased the number of some particular tribes of them, that, like an overgrown standing army, they have become formidable to the Government and upon many occasions intimidate the legislature. . . . The Member of Parliament who supports every proposal for strengthening this monopoly, is sure to acquire not only the reputation of understanding trade, but great popularity and influence with an order of men whose numbers and wealth render them of great importance."[3] Nor did Adam Smith hesitate to pour scorn on the merchant class, representing them as powerful coteries, who used the economic dogma of self-sufficiency to shape the policies of government and line their own pockets. "Of the greater part of the regulations concerning colonial trade, the merchants who carry it on, it must be observed, have been the principal advisers. We must not wonder then, if in the greater part of

[1] *Three Discourses*. Republished in 1787 in connection with the Treaty of Commerce with France.

[2] *Wealth of Nations* (ed. E. Cannan), Vol. II, p. 109.

[3] *Ibid.*, Vol. I, pp. 435–6; see also pp. 457–8.

them, their interest has been more considered than either that of the colonies or the Mother Country."[1]

But Adam Smith and the " œconomists " had little influence on the parliamentary public opinion of the time, for they were running exactly counter to it. The people of the Mother Country believed that their sacrifices in blood and treasure were repaid by a veritable gold mine in the monopoly of trade.[2] In a satirical diatribe against the monied interest, Smith partially explains his own failure. " To found a great empire for the sole purpose of raising up a people of customers may at first sight appear a project fit only for a nation of shop-keepers, but extremely fit for a nation whose government is influenced by shop-keepers. Such statesmen and such statesmen alone are capable of fancying that they will find some advantage in employing the blood and treasure of their fellow-citizens."

[1] *Ibid.*, p. 85.

[2] Nicholson, J. S., *A project of Empire.*

When the French traveller, Grosley, asked an Englishman in Drury Lane whether he considered bread at 3*d.* a pound and beer at 3*d.* half a pot worthy trophies of the struggle which closed in 1763, he was answered that it did not matter. " *We have got Canada and beaver.*" Quoted by Hertz, G. B., *The Old Colonial System*, p. 66.

CHAPTER II

THE EXPEDIENCY OF THE QUEBEC ACT[1]

In 1763 the Peace of Paris had officially terminated the Seven Years' War, and provided for the cession of Canada to Great Britain. From October of that year until May of 1775 a royal proclamation formed the constitution,[2] or basis of administration, in the province of Quebec. As an instrument of government it was one of the most ineffective in the history of British colonial rule; and for ten years it became the studious endeavour of successive British governments to repair its omissions and correct its errors.

The original object of the Proclamation had been to confine European settlement to the seaboard by means of a well-defined boundary line, which should afford barrier protection to the Indians and to the all-important fur trade of the western country.[3] Unfortunately, before the measure was pushed through Parliament, the President of the Board of Trade, Lord Hillsborough, hastily appended other provisions which proved to be of most doubtful relevance. In brief, these additions defined boundaries and established similar forms of civil government in the four strangely dissimilar territories of Quebec, East Florida, West Florida and Grenada.

In so far as Quebec was concerned, the Proclamation created a province out of what was really the inhabited portion of New France along the River St. Lawrence. It provided for the executive government of the province by means of a governor and council, with the proviso that a general assembly should be called, " so soon as the state and circumstances of the said colonies will admit thereof." Lastly, legislative power

[1] A paper read before the Cambridge Historical Society on March 5, 1929.

[2] Established as such by Lord Mansfield, in Campbell *vs.* Hall, 1774. See Kennedy, W. P. M., *Documents of the Canadian Constitution, 1759–1915*, pp. 79–85.

[3] See Alvord, C. W., *Mississippi Valley in British Politics*, Ch. VII, *passim*.

was granted to the governor, acting in conjunction with the council and assembly. The question of legislating without the consent of the assembly was left unanswered, other than by a clause, which smugly declared that until an assembly should be called, "subjects might resort to and enjoy the benefit of the laws of the Realm." To facilitate the apportioning of this blessing, Courts of Justice were to be immediately established, in which all causes were to be determined, "as may be agreeable to the laws of England." This most significant of the articles implied apparently the total abolition of French law.

The Proclamation was silent on the question of religion; but by the Treaty of Paris the new Roman Catholic subjects were granted the privilege of freedom of worship, according to the rites of the Romish Church, "as far as the laws of Great Britain permit." Yet the Test and Toleration Acts were still in force in England. Might they not perchance apply in Canada? Furthermore, might tithes and other dues be legally collected as under the French regime?

All these questions and doubts confronted British ministries and colonial administrators until 1774. In the meantime, they were met by a sort of rough and ready compromise. If the Proclamation, in the words of Mansfield, was among the most rash and unjust of any acts in history,[1] the governors of Canada[2] were determined to temper its severity; if it seemed to inaugurate a policy of repression, they were determined to bend it into one of conciliation.

The subject of boundaries was a matter for the home authorities to settle in their own good time. The matter of a legislative assembly was shelved. Despite the rebellious agitations of the mercantile element, both Governor Murray and Governor Carleton were opposed to the establishment of what, under the laws of England, would have been no more than an English merchant oligarchy.[3] As to freedom of religion, the con-

[1] Mansfield to Grenville, *The Grenville Papers* (W. J. Smith, ed.), London, 1852, Vol. II, p. 477.

[2] General James Murray, 1763–68; Sir Guy Carleton, Lieutenant-Governor, 1766–8; Governor, 1768–74.

[3] Shortt and Doughty, *Documents relating to the Constitutional History of Canada*, 1759–91, Vol. I, p. 295. Carleton wrote to Shelburne on Jan. 20, 1768, with regard to English petitioners: "I had no objection to assemblies in General, yet such was the peculiar situation of Canada . . . I

querors were pledged by the terms of the capitulation in 1760 to grant full toleration of the Roman Catholic religion.[1] The Treaty of Paris had added—" as far as the laws of Great Britain permit," but Murray declared that he would resign if the penal laws were enforced against " the best and bravest race upon the globe."[2] In 1765, he referred the question of Roman Catholic status to the home government. To his satisfaction, the Attorney-General and the Solicitor-General were able to report that His Majesty's Roman Catholic subjects are not " subject in those colonies to the incapacities, disabilities and penalties to which Roman Catholics in this kingdom are subject by the Laws thereof."[3] This kindly policy of religious concession was further developed in the following year, when permission was given for the consecration of a bishop. Although Mgr. Briand was legally titled " Superintendent of the Roman Catholic church in Canada ", he was in reality Bishop of Quebec.

But of the multitude of problems pressing for solution, the question of the law of the province loomed largest. How could the country be saved from the uncertainty and confusion which would inevitably follow so drastic a revolution as the abandonment of French law ? Again, the expedient adopted was one of compromise. Murray of his own accord admitted French Canadians as jurors into the Court of King's Bench ; in the Court of Common Pleas French Canadian advocates were allowed to practise, and French laws and customs were to be allowed in all cases between French Canadians that had arisen before October 1, 1764.[4] The British Government gave immediate and definite indication of their intention to support Murray in his work of conciliation. In 1764, additional instructions were forwarded to the Governor in order to

could hit off no plan that was not liable to many Inconveniences and some Danger."

[1] Articles of Capitulation, Montreal, Sept. 8, 1760. Article XXVII : " The free exercise of the Catholic Apostolic and Roman Religion shall subsist entire. . . ." Answer : " Granted, as to the free exercise of their religion. The obligation of paying tithes to the Priests will depend on the King's pleasure." Shortt and Doughty, *op. cit.*, I, 25.

[2] Kennedy, W. P. M., *op. cit.*, p. 40.

[3] Report of Norton and De Grey, Lincoln's Inn, June 10, 1765 ; Shortt and Doughty, *op. cit.*, I, 236.

[4] Wallace, W. S., " The Beginnings of British Rule in Canada," *Canadian Historical Review*, 1925, p. 213.

remove, as they declared, " the misconstruction of the proclamation of 7th October, 1763." British laws and constitution should apply where " the lives and liberties " of all subjects are concerned, but " shall not operate to take away from the native Inhabitants the benefit of their own Laws and Customs in Cases where Titles to Land and the Modes of Descent, Alienation and Settlement are in question, nor to preclude them from that share in the Administration of Judicature, which both in Reason and Justice, they are intitled to in Common with the rest of our Subjects."[1] In July, 1766, these instructions were given statutory force by way of an ordinance which permitted French Canadian jurors to sit and French Canadian lawyers to plead in any court in the colony;[2] and by an ordinance of 1767 which definitely established the French laws and customs concerning Tenure, Inheritance and Alienation of Lands.[3]

For the majority of people, this was the only law and custom that really mattered, because it was almost the only type with which they came in frequent contact. Only among certain classes was there recourse to commercial law; and in this, the greatest confusion prevailed. At first, the French naturally preferred the old French custom, and in the Court of Common Pleas, a large discretionary power was exercised through liberal interpretations of the cases in question. But gradually, as the benefits of English law became known, there developed a hybrid creation of French Canadian custom and English law. Attorney-General Maseres, who made, at the Government's request, an impartial examination of this diversity, remarks in conclusion—" Thus, it appears that in many respects the Canadians apprehend the laws of England to be in force in this province, and that they endeavour to apply them and put them in practice whenever they take them to be for their advantage; though in other points, and particularly in those of inheritance and dower, and the distribution of the effects of persons who die intestate, they have universally adhered to their former laws and usages."[4] What was at first

[1] Canadian Archives, Dartmouth Papers, M383, p. 50; Shortt and Doughty, *op. cit.*, p. 225, Note I.

[2] Wallace, W. S., *op. cit.*, p. 215; Kennedy, W. P. M., *op. cit.*, pp. 48–9.

[3] Shortt and Doughty, *op. cit.*, I, 292–4.

[4] To the Earl of Hillsborough, A Draught of An Intended Report of the

only moderately appreciated, came in time to be preferred; and this strange conglomerate of English law and French custom began to knit itself into a sort of Common Law. It may not have been wholly intelligible to either judges or advocates; but there is no evidence to show that it existed with any great demur on the part of the new subjects.

In the meantime, the whole problem of civil laws was being investigated by the home government. During Rockingham's short ministry, it was referred to Attorney-General Yorke and Solicitor-General de Grey,[1] who encouraged the definite building up of a French English system along those mingling lines of old custom and modern English procedure. Their recommendations, put in force, would have given legal sanction to the policy of compromise; but a sudden change of Ministry prevented any action being taken.

The most conscientious attempt to solve the puzzle was made by Lord Shelburne, as Secretary of State for the Southern Department in the Chatham Ministry. He called for thorough investigation and report from the Governor, Sir Guy Carleton, Chief Justice Hey and Attorney-General Maseres. As it happened, the Attorney-General was finally left to frame the joint report himself. Francis Maseres was a distinguished graduate and fellow of Clare College, Cambridge. He was called to the Bar in 1758, and after eight unsatisfactory years in law, accepted the post of Attorney-General in Canada. He was a prolific writer; but perhaps the most important work in his long career of authorship was this report on the state of the laws and administration, occupying some fifty closely printed pages.[2] In it, he displayed a moderation and judgment singularly out of keeping with the usual propagandist manner of writing in that day, and without that strong anti-Catholic bias which was later to warp so finely balanced a mind.

Maseres gave a clear analysis of the situation as he found it, emphasizing particularly the uncertainty of the laws, and the

Honourable the Governor-in-Chief and the Council of the Province of Que. to the King, concerning the State of the Laws and the Administration of Justice in that Province; Que., Sept. 11, 1769; Shortt and Doughty, *op. cit.*, I. 346.

[1] Report regarding the Civil Government of Quebec, April 4, 1766; Shortt and Doughty, I. 251.

[2] "To the Earl of Hillsborough . . ." etc. See above.

lack of any definite idea as to what sort of law was in force. To remedy the evil, he suggested four methods. First, an entirely new code, excluding both the laws of England and France. This would receive its main opposition from the French Canadians, who would deprecate any attempt to "lose" the custom of Paris. Furthermore, there would be interminable work in compiling such a code. On the other hand, it would satisfy the English inhabitants by removing the old edicts and customs of Paris, and it would also cut one of the bonds which bound the French to the old land with its old traditions. The second method, that of reviving the whole French law and introducing by ordinance only a few of the laws of England seemed the shortest and easiest; yet it would disgust and enrage the English merchants and solidify French nationalism more strongly than ever. The third method, that of using the laws of England as a general basis and permitting the Canadian customs to continue with respect to excepted subjects, was Maseres' favourite plan. The fourth method involved the making of the law of England the general law of the land with the exception of special ordinances maintaining old French customs in special cases. This last he felt would not satisfy the French.

Apparently Maseres owed his Canadian appointment in great part to the influence of the British mercantile party.[1] Consequently, his emphasis on the English law did not coincide with the views of the aristocratic Carleton. His own solution—the third alternative—favoured the continuance of the policy of compromise, which Murray had initiated and which the Attorney- and Solicitor-Generals had recommended. But Carleton had already made up his mind to abandon the middle way of compromise, and in his special report he recommended the French civil law in its entirety. From this recommendation Maseres dissented; and in a criticism of the Governor's report, he re-emphasized the value and expediency of a system of civil law, retaining only that part of the French law which related to land tenure, inheritance and dower.[2]

By 1770 these conflicting reports had reached London. They were referred by Lord Hillsborough, Shelburne's successor

[1] Wallace, W. S., *op. cit.*, p. 208.
[2] Kennedy, *op. cit.*, pp. 58–61.

as Secretary for the Southern Department, to the legal advisers of the Crown, who in "lengthy and learned documents" added their opinions to the plethora of varying evidence. Attorney-General Thurlow and Solicitor-General Wedderburn, in contradiction to their predecessors, leaned to the ideas of Carleton;[1] Chief Justice Hey and Advocate-General Marriott to those of Maseres.

The Quebec Act has often been considered as the fruits of their long negotiation, as the joint product of many minds. But it represented too great a break with continuous, harmonious development to be that. Maseres' advocacy of compromise following directly as it did on a policy which Murray had initiated, which observant law officers had recommended and which successive British ministries had definitely encouraged, went unavailing. The Quebec Act bore indelibly the stamp of one man—Carleton. Only in minor ways did it resemble the view of some of his more understanding contemporaries.

The Bill was introduced into the Lords on May 2, 1774, and came into force in May of the following year. The provisions may be summed up briefly as follows. The boundaries of the province should be extended to include the western hinterland between the Ohio and Mississippi and the northern country up to the frontiers of the Hudson's Bay territory. Since it was deemed "inexpedient to call an Assembly," a legislative council should be appointed by the King. This body would have power to conduct all affairs in the province except taxation; and there was to be no religious test for membership. The Roman Catholics were to enjoy the free exercise of their religion subject to the supremacy of the King, and their clergy were to receive their accustomed dues and rights. All disputes as to property and civil rights were in future to be determined in accordance with the laws and customs of Canada, unless "varied or altered" by ordinance of the Governor and Council. The Proclamation of 1763, so far as it applied to Canada, together with all commissions and ordinances relative to civil government and administration of justice issued in pursuance of its terms, was revoked.[2]

[1] See Shortt and Doughty, *op. cit.*, I, 424–83.
[2] Coupland, R., *The Quebec Act*, p. 91.

Twelve years after the event, Carleton, now Lord Dorchester, remarked to the Secretary of State, Sydney, " The Quebec Act was introduced at a time when nothing could be thought of but self-defence."[1] As in the case of the Proclamation, the Ministry were in haste. We know very little that went on behind the scenes during that crowded year. The Commons never viewed or heard the reports on the situation, and gained their information solely from party literature or fragmentary testimonies at the bar of the House. The Quebec Act was passed in the heat of impending strife, and was an instinctive act of self-defence.

Many historians in the past have accepted Governor Haldimand's words, that the Bill was aimed at preventing the Americans getting possession of the continent.[2] By providing for a barrier extension of French Canada into the vast hinterland between the Mississippi and the Ohio, the westward expansion of the colonies might be checked and perchance their revolutionary ardour dampened. It is beyond the scope of this paper to discuss the problem of Indian protection and American expansion. Suffice it to say, the boundary clause was the result of a long-considered policy which was not inspired by commercial interests alone, and not largely affected by conditions in the other colonies. At the time when the provisions of the Bill were first discussed, rebellion was regarded as a much less serious matter than war with France.[3] Had it not been for French intrigues and propaganda and the constant probability of the renewal of war, with Canada as a stake, it is reasonable to say that the Quebec Act would not have represented so complete a reversal of policy. Wise statesmen knew that the Treaty of Paris was only a truce.[4] The trails of French conspiracy were too conspicuous to be disregarded. Carleton, whose views so predominated in the determination of the provisions of the Quebec Act, seemed to be completely absorbed

[1] Dorchester to Sydney, June 13, 1787; C.O. 42/50, No. 17.

[2] See Justin Winsor, *American Historical Review*, pp. 439–40 of Vol. I.

[3] Professor Coupland in his *Quebec Act* has been the first to give this fundamental fact its true emphasis.

[4] In the Public Record Office is a long document, unsigned, but in the handwriting of the Jesuit, Pierre Ribaud, and probably written about 1763 or 1764. It is entitled " L'Etat Actuel du Canada," and gives a fairly detailed survey of the resources of the country, and their possible value to France. It urges the necessity of a reconquest; and was obviously intended for Choiseul's consumption. See C.O. 5/43.

by the fear of French invasion. "I can have no doubt," he wrote secretly to Hillsborough, "that France as soon as she is determined to begin a war will attempt to regain Canada."[1] In 1771, during his stay in England, he prepared a memorandum as to the means to be adopted against possible French attack. He declared that the regaining of Canada, though not lucrative, would be most advantageous to France on account of the strong foothold it would give her on the North American continent.[2] Marriott who already sensed danger in Carleton's proposals with regard to the Civil Laws, felt forced to remark that if Canada should be recovered by France in a future period by the mere want of wisdom in a British government, and "if France or any other power should obtain but a near equality of force at sea, the consequence must prove the conquest of all our American colonies, or perhaps, the establishment of a new independent empire upon a general revolt of all the colonies, of which Canada by its position would form the head."[3]

The Quebec Act was, therefore, primarily intended as an expedient to save Canada, an act of conciliation to wean the French as far as possible from their old allegiance. But, was such a complete reversal of the Proclamation of 1763 and the total abandonment of the policy of compromise either expedient or effective? Certain historians declare that it was. They contend that if the policy of the Quebec Act had not been adopted, Canada would have been lost to the British Empire

[1] Carleton to Hillsborough, Que., Nov. 20, 1768 (secret); C.O. 42/28. See also Carleton to Hillsborough, Que., Jan. 18, 1769; C.O. 42/29; Carleton to Shelburne, Nov. 25, 1767; C.O. 47/110. In this letter he speaks of Canadian-born officers who served in the last war, "who are now in a particular manner cantoned in Touraine and supported by the French government."

Note also Hillsborough to Lieut-Governor Cramahé (separate and secret), April 9, 1771, Whitehall; C.O. 42/31, and Wm. Johnson to John Blackburn, Johnson Hall, Jan. 20, 1774, regarding French intrigues with Indians; Add. MS. 24323, Brit. Mus.

[2] Cramahé to (Hillsborough ?), Que., June 30, 1774; C.O. 43/13, fol. 127. In an earlier connection, note, Egremont to Murray, Whitehall, Aug. 13, 1763: "His Majesty has reason to suspect that the French may be disposed to avail themselves of the liberty of the Catholic religion granted to the inhabitants to keep up their connection with France, and to induce them to join for the recovery of their country. The priests must therefore be narrowly watched and anyone who meddles in civil affairs be removed." C.O. 42/24.

[3] Plan of a Code of Laws for the Province of Quebec, London, 1771; Shortt and Doughty, *op. cit.*, I, 459.

in 1775, and no distinct Canadian nation could ever have come into being.[1]

It is difficult to estimate justly the Quebec Act, because it is so easy to deliver patronizing judgments in retrospect. One tends to forget that statesmen are always limited by the circumstances of the time, and must needs devote all their energies to meeting the wants of the day. At this time, the once despised Canada was now regarded as worth saving in itself, and that, at the expense of destroying the structure which had been slowly building up since 1763. The Advocate-General had maintained that " after certain new regulations have been submitted with patience by His Majesty's new Canadian subjects for a space of twelve years, though with some such complaining as is natural upon a change of masters, the foundation which has been laid for an approximation to the Manners and foundation of the new Sovereign Country must either continue to be built upon or otherwise the whole that has been done must be thrown down."[2] The Quebec Act represented the tearing down process, and its authors regarded the sacrifice as just and necessary.

The Proclamation of 1763 had operated to abolish the old French laws and to give the colony the " benefit of the laws of England." The injustice and absurdity of this plan had been obvious from the outset ; and we have noted the slow growth of a middle path, the system of conciliation by compromise, inaugurated by the colonial governors and supported by the British governments. On the whole, French Canada appeared satisfied.[3] Then, at one stroke, the Bill of 1774

[1] Cf. Coupland, R., *The Quebec Act*, p. 194.

[2] Marriott, *op. cit.*, *passim.*

[3] Choiseul had sent Baron Kalb to America in 1768 to investigate the probability of a revolt against England, and of its success if attempted. During his sojourn, Kalb paid a visit to Canada, from whence he made reports not likely to warm the heart of the foreign minister. " There were few inhabitants," he said, " who retained their affection for the old French régime." " Under the British, their lands had increased in value, their taxes were less and they enjoyed unconditional freedom of conscience." See Friederich Kapp, *Leben des Americanischen Generals,—Johann Kalb;* Stuttgart, 1862 ; London, 1912.

An unsigned memoir among the *Documents relating to the Colonial History of New York*, throws further light upon ambitions and their blight. Referring to the impossibility of exciting a rebellion in Canada, the writer speaks of the people as having been further drawn from their allegiance to France by the " mild régime of the English, the latter in their policy having neglected nothing to expedite the return of that comfort and liberty." Vol. X, p. 1155. (1763.)

destroyed the work of the past few years, and restored in their entirety the French civil laws and customs, without the safeguards of English commercial law, Habeas Corpus, or trial by jury. It involved a return of the arbitrary feudal system with its autocratic seigneurial relationships, from which the habitant had gradually and apparently gladly broken away. It brought the trade of the Lower St. Lawrence under the ancient French laws long since obsolete in France itself, and stultified the commerce of that region for generations. The main virtue of the Quebec Act was the legal recognition of the Roman Catholic religion, which Britain was in honour bound to grant according to the terms of the Capitulation in 1760. Yet this was accompanied by a clause which permitted the compulsory collection of tithes.

It was not altogether strange, therefore, that the habitant should feel some apprehension with regard to the return of the old oppressive subjections, which he inevitably associated with Land and Church. His conduct before and after the passing of the Quebec Act indicates decisively that the change of régime in 1760, in so far as it implied a release from military and judicial subjection, was appreciated by the masses of the population. For twelve years the habitant had tasted freedom, and had begun to resent the restrictive authority of priest and seigneur, whose power outside the little feudal world had sadly languished. As Carleton remarked to Dartmouth shortly after the Bill came into force, " The gentry and the clergy have been very useful, but both have lost much of their influence."[1] This was mainly true of the seigneurs. The better part of them had sold their estates and returned to France following after the cession of Canada in 1763.[2] Both Murray and Carleton had tried hard to maintain the old social status of the remainder, but, poor in numbers and wealth, they were no longer in any sense a governing class.[3] Lieutenant-Governor Cramahé speaks of their fading prestige in a letter to Hillsborough of July, 1772. " Far from complaining of slavery, the Canadian *noblesse* allege that from the present freedom, the

[1] C.O. 42/35.

[2] The *Journal* of the Legislative Council for July 2, 1773, contains references to 43 petitions for seigneuries by individuals, mainly Scotch and English; See C.O. 45/3.

[3] See Munro, W.B., *Seigneurs of Old Canada*, Chap. VII, *passim*.

middling and lower classes are losing respect for their superiors."[1] With an allusion to Carleton's influence on the formulation of the Quebec Act, Chief Justice Hey wrote to the Lord Chancellor in June of 1775, and referred to the Governor's "injudicious dealings with the seigneurs . . . the[ir] elation at the supposed restoration of their old privileges has given just offence to their own people and to the English merchants."[2]

The influence of the clergy had been great, and was still a force to be counted; but it was greatly weakened by the provision which had again laid on the people the burden of obnoxious compulsory tithes.[3] Furthermore, there were schisms in their ranks, between the French clergy and the Canadian, the priests of the old country regarding their colonial-born brethren with no small measure of contempt.[4] According to Cramahé, the French clergy favoured a change of rule and might lead the inhabitants, whereas the Canadian were strongly interested to prevent such a reversal, and threw their influence into the opposing scale.[5] Yet, within three years, even they had recanted of their loyalty.[6]

But the true test of the expediency of the Quebec Act was to be its effectiveness in preserving French Canadian loyalty during the American rebellion. A year of civil strife had not gone by before this measure of conciliation began to produce results strangely in opposition to its purpose. While Carleton without men or money faced upheaval within his own province and attack from the south, he was receiving letters from Dartmouth, Secretary for the Colonies, asking for troops to reinforce

[1] Que., July 25, 1772; C.O. 42/31.

[2] C.O. 42/35.

[3] Lord Sheffield notes in his *Observations*, etc.: "Their [the Canadian] priests acknowledge that they have in great measure lost their influence."

[4] Cramahé to Hillsborough, July 25, 1772; C.O. 42/31.

[5] *Ibid.*

[6] On Sept. 14, 1779, Haldimand wrote a "secret and confidential" despatch to the Secretary of State. He declared that "the clergy who in general behaved so well in 1775 and 1776, since the French alliance with the Rebel colonies, are cooled very much to the British interests; that those among them who are natives of France should lean to that side is not after all so surprising, but that the Canadian priests who have already reaped so much advantage by the change and have a chance for still greater, having ever been kept under while under the French government, is extraordinary, and can only be accounted for in this way, that as they are for the most part taken out of the lowest class of people, they are fully as ignorant and as void of principle as those from whom they originate"; C.O. 43/14, fol. 203.

Gage at New York.[1] At the time when the introduction of the old militia conscript system[2] seemed to imply the return of all the exactions of an *ancien régime* with its *lettres de cachet*, John Dickinson at Philadelphia was drafting a conciliatory address to be generously distributed for the benefit of the disaffected on the St. Lawrence. There was indeed a strong neutral element, particularly among the ecclesiastical and the professional classes. Only to the south of the St. Lawrence did General Montgomery gain recruits. Nevertheless, the attitude in general revealed for the edification of the colonial authorities the quite unexpected sequel to the Quebec Act. The great body of French Canadians, despite the often zealous exertions of priest or seigneur, refused to submit to the feudal authority of the *noblesse* under the restored system. Chief Justice Hey expressed judicial horror and surprise in a letter to the Lord Chancellor—" What will be Your Lordship's astonishment, when I tell you that an Act passed for the express purpose of gratifying the Canadians and which was supposed to comprehend all that they either wished or wanted is become the first object of their discontent and dislike. English officers to command them in time of war and English laws to govern them in time of peace is the general wish." And again—" they are terrified and corrupted to a degree that Your Lordship can have no idea of, and are impressed with the strangest ideas that ever entered into the minds of men."[3] The letters and documents of the time literally abound in similar statements reflecting the strong objections manifested by the mass of French Canadians at being subjected again to feudal domination.[4] Fourteen years of British rule had worked a revolution in their attitude toward authority, and their conduct following the passing of the Quebec Act shows strikingly to what extent they had become reconciled to the less oppressive, less dictatorial British law and administration. From all evidence it would appear that it was a real dread of the restoration of old

[1] On July 1, he wrote urging the raising of 3,000 Canadian troops; on July 24, he increased the request to 6,000.

[2] Proclamation of Carleton, June 9, 1775.

[3] Chief Justice Hey to the Lord Chancellor (Thurlow), Que., Aug. 28, 1775; Shortt and Doughty, *op. cit.*, I, 670.

[4] See Carleton to Dartmouth, Que., June 7, 1775; Shortt and Doughty, *op. cit.*, I, 663. Cramahé to Dartmouth, Que., Sept. 21, 1775; *ibid.*, p. 667. General Burgoyne to Germaine, May 14, 1777; *ibid.*, p. 677.

institutions, of the revival of the authority of the seigneur and the exacting paternalism of the Church, which made so many French Canadians openly rebel against the militia laws and sullenly refuse to assist the seigneurs in defence.[1] To a certain extent the slight upper stratum of French society was won over, and for the time being the clergy, but generally speaking, the Canadians were not kept loyal. The Quebec Act " aggravated rather than captivated " the " emancipated habitant," and made him an easy mark for the shafts of American propagandists.

Carleton, as he himself admitted, vastly overestimated the interest of the French Canadians in the struggle. They had no reason to love Great Britain, but they had less reason to love the British American colonies, who had been their particular hereditary foes during all the frightful border wars of the eighteenth century. Their leaders must have known that an American conquest, despite all its promises of relief from " feudal chains of vassalage "[2] would mean the extinction of the French Canadian mode of life. As a mere matter of self-interest, the British Crown was the French Canadians' best protection, the guardian of his Church, his vital laws and customs, his peculiar traditions. No violent reversal of policy was necessary to secure that protection. It had been secured already under the policy of toleration and compromise. " It is necessary," said Marriott, " to make the Canadians forget that they were Frenchmen and to approximate them more as British Canadians to a British government by a Middle system, so as to effect what the Chief Justice calls—' the happy Temperament of New and Old Laws.' "[1] This middle system the authors of the Quebec Act rejected on the grounds of expediency. With a will to be generous, they attempted to revive the defunct spirit of the past. But the new régime of complex laws could never give energy to functions which had responded to the paternal hand of the French *Intendant* within a French feudal system. The fragile skeleton of " old authority " had been restored ; but the spirit which gave life had gone for ever.

[1] The military ordinance of Mar. 29, 1777, enforced the corvée labour, which became the subject of many grievous petitions and even open hostility. C.O. 45/4.

[2] Advertisement of Nov. 26, 1777 ; C.O. 45/8.

CHAPTER III

THE WAR PERIOD, 1776–82

THE negotiations preceding the Treaty of Paris had shown Canada to be the pawn of party politics and an object of some small ridicule. But, if the colony had been almost carelessly won in 1763, the exigencies of a war situation eleven years later revealed the definite wish of the British Government to retain possession.

Fear of France was the dominating factor in British foreign policy from 1763 to 1778. This attitude reacted on British policy towards Canada in a singularly vital way. The Quebec Act of 1774, which restored the involved French civil laws and an arbitrary feudal system and gave legal recognition to the Roman Catholic religion, was an expedient chiefly intended to wean the Canadians as far as possible from their old allegiance. Pure necessity became the law at the expense of conscience. In other words, the main motive which actuated the minds of statesmen to give back to the French their old feudal government, and which enabled George III to grant religious freedom to an alien faith, was not one of altruistic generosity, but fundamentally the desire " to retain what had been won."

In the period between 1763 and 1774, Canada had in some small degree managed to justify the predictions of her friendly advocates, Shelburne and Shirley. The Quebec Act, in so far as it was an attempt to retain the colony within the Empire, represents the first upward trend in the value of the country in the eyes of the mercantilists at home. It was of course a modest gain, based almost wholly on an appreciation of the fur trade and fisheries. Canadians, according to a pamphleteer estimate, did not take from Britain more than the value of

17*s.* 6*d.* for each inhabitant; "consequently this colony has the appearance of being little profitable; but when we consider the principal part of their export consists in an advantageous staple, peltry, it is not, though far north, without its use to this country."[1]

But responsible men had continued to find further advantages in the possession of so northern a province. Hillsborough, whose former errors as President of the Board of Trade[2] did not blind his contemporaries to past experience and present knowledge, saw "great and solid advantages arising to the commerce and navigation of this kingdom from North America, depending principally upon giving proper encouragement to the fishery, to the production of naval stores and to the supply of the Sugar Islands with lumber and provisions."[3]

A short time later, Advocate-General Marriott reported to his government that in spite of the natural indolence and ignorance of the people, and their present poverty, and the fact that the St. Lawrence was frozen for six months in the year and was full of dangerous rocks and shoals, "yet when we consider the prodigious increase of population, the exceeding fertility of Montreal, the healthiness of the air and the vast woods of Canada, capable of supplying naval stores and lumber for the West Indies and for the Mother Country, the product of horned cattle, sheep, horses, hogs, wool, corn, hemp, flax, furs, potash, iron, etc., and the situation of the River St. Lawrence so adapted to the fishery and increase of seamen, objects little pursued by the French Government, . . . it is reasonable to think that all these circumstances will in course of time conspire to make Quebec the St. Petersburg of North America."[4]

But many obstacles barred the attainment of Marriott's ideal. One great difficulty was the traditional inertia of a

[1] *Essays Commercial and Political*, 1777. (Brit. Mus.)—The writer adds that "the f[illegible] trade is the most essential benefit—next to the fisheries—which we can reap from Northern Settlements," p. 74.

[2] See above, p. 18.

[3] Hillsborough to Gage, Whitehall, July 31, 1770. C.O. 5/241, 315 *et seq.*, also C.O. 5/88, 199.

[4] From the report—"*A code of Law Civil and Criminal for the Province of Quebec, by order of the King,*" July 31, 1772, C.O. 47/110 and Shortt and Doughty, *op. cit.*, I, p. 440. Marriott makes frequent reference to Abbé Raynal's *Histoire philosophique et politique des établissements et du commerce des Européens dans les deux Indes,*" 1770.

people, utterly unacquainted with the language, religion or mode of government of their conquerors. Another lay in the past policy of the French Government. Under the "ancien régime" commerce had been confined almost entirely to furs. Some small trade in fish and lumber had existed with the French islands, but the amount was inconsiderable.[1] Agriculture remained practically at a standstill. Habitants whom adventurous instincts did not take to the woods, still tilled the long narrow strips of farm land which bordered the St. Lawrence from Montreal to Gaspée, but the fruits were meagre. Only rarely were large surpluses eked from these ribboned farms, for methods of agriculture were obsolete as in old France, and the seigneur gave little more encouragement than immediate interest requires.[2] Nor did the French Government contribute greatly, either by way of bounties or instruction. With far-reaching political dreams and aspirations they paid even less attention to dull earth than did the seigneurs.[3] The Intendant or Governor generally fixed the price of such commodities as wheat and provisions, but often at such low rates that progressive tillage was discouraged.[4]

The Treaty of Paris brought about a change of masters and the end of this barnacled feudal system. Grants of land in free and common socage superseded those "en seigneurie" or "en censive" until the Quebec Act reversed the system again. But the Canada of 1774 could have changed but little in outward appearance. Although the majority of the *noblesse* had left the colony, Council Minutes reveal the large numbers of seigneurial holdings which fell to Scotch or English hands.[5] Unfortunately the new settlers were mainly specula-

[1] *Board of Trade Report* (a review), Jan. 24, 1781; *Acts of the Privy Council, Colonial*, Vol. VI, p. 580, No. 1001.

[2] *Ibid.*

[3] Advocate-General Marriott declared that even the fur trade was but a small object of attention in proportion to political views. "The great use of the colony was offensively: as a place of arms, to form the head of a chain of forts and to harass the British colonies, and, by its position and communication with the lakes quite down to the Mississippi, to command the commerce and force of the whole interior of the vast American continent. (Contained in *Plan of a Code of Laws for the Province of Quebec*, London, 1774.) Shortt and Doughty, Vol. I, p. 458; C.O. 47/110.

[4] *Memorandum of Adam Lymburner*, Feb. 9, 1788. C.O. 42/12, fol. 239, also *Board of Trade Report*, B.T. 5/5, fols. 35–6.

[5] See *Council Minutes*, Quebec, July 2, 1773.

tors, who purchased these seigneuries at sacrifice prices. They were good investments, for most of the estates included extensive grants of uncleared lands, which with the increase of the colony would gradually rise in value ;[1] but their owners were not the type to lay the foundation of an agricultural community. Britain still found her most zealous representatives in the Scotch and English-American trading class, and their principal concern was the fur trade.

Progress was therefore bound to be slow. Yet under the circumstances it was astonishing. From 1771 to 1775 the Government was fully supplied with the flour and produce of the province. On an annual average for those same years, the export of wheat was about 265,000 bushels ; flour, 1700 barrels ; biscuits, 2000 barrels ; and peas, 2400 bushels,[2] mainly to Nova Scotia and Newfoundland. Although distance placed her at a serious disadvantage, Canada had also been able to carry on a small trade with the British West India Islands, mainly in flour, wheat, cod-fish and biscuit, as well as varieties of wood for making casks or building houses.[3] According to Edward Long, the annual export of supplies to the West Indies, during the period 1771–3 averaged under £4000 sterling—" about equal," he added contemptuously, " to the purchase of 350 puncheons of Jamaica rum." On the other hand, for the same period, the Atlantic coast colonies had provided the West Indies with supplies to the annual value of over a million sterling, which thus made the Canadian share of the trade equal to less than one two hundred and fiftieth of the whole.[4]

[1] Munro, W. B., *The Seigneurial System in Canada*, p. 192.

[2] *Acts of Privy Council, Col*, Vol. VI, (The Unbound Papers), p. 580. According to Adam Lymburner, in 1774 nearly 450,000 lbs. of wheat, besides large quantities of flour and biscuit was shipped. C.O. 42/12, fol. 239. Also note evidence of former Inspector-General Irving, March 30, 1784, with regard to imports and exports in North America. Considerable beef and pork was shipped to the British West Indies between 1771 and 1773, and Irving believed " there is a probability of Canada and Nova Scotia being able to furnish a large supply in a short time." B.T. 5/1, fols. 90–97.

[3] See Appendix A.

[4] Such disproportion elicited this ironic response from Edward Long, " Whatever your North American has predicted of the eventual grandeur, population and ability of Canada and N.S., he must certainly be aware that the inhabitants of our West India Islands (amounting to half a million souls) will not bear to be kept upon rations of refuse, cod-fish and a short allowance of musty bread for years to come, until the golden epoch of that grandeur

Owing to the fact that Board of Trade statistics of clearances from Quebec regularly include the West Indies with " Southern parts of Europe and Africa," it is difficult to ascertain accurately the extent of this commerce. Such inclusive figures, however, provide a general confirmation of Long's estimate. In 1772, out of 1208 vessels with lumber and provisions arriving in the West Indies from North America, only thirteen were from the three northern colonies, Canada, Nova Scotia, and Newfoundland ; and of these apparently only five were from Canada.[1] In 1774, sixty-seven vessels sailed from Quebec in the South European, African, West Indian category ; but in 1778, the number was reduced to thirteen[2] and continued to dwindle until the end of the war.[3]

Nevertheless, it is apparent that until the beginning of the war Canadian agriculture had made astonishing progress. A comparison of trade statistics down to 1775 reveals a similar growth of commerce in natural products of the farm and forest. Prospects were bright for a continuance of this prosperity, until the invasion of 1775 put a stop to most trade long before the season finished.[4] The governor was forced to commission all hands by proclamation to transport provisions, undertake road

and ability dawn on their horizon. Your North American says we should wait events rather than endeavour to force them. But, Sir, a hundred years is an unconsiderable time to wait for a Bellyful. . . ." Edward Long, *Observations on West Indies Trade,* (Brit. Mus.) Add. MS. 18274.

[1] *Board of Trade Minutes,* B.T. 5/1, fol. 11.

[2] C.O. 42/10 ; see Appendix A. Note in this regard, former Inspector-General Irving's report in *Board of Trade Minutes,* B.T. 5/1, fols. 90–106.

[3] See Add. MS. 21861 for a list of ships to Quebec from (1) Great Britain, West Indies and America ; (2) Clearances ; (3) Cargoes, i.e. exports and imports to Quebec, 1768–83.

[4] On March 18, 1784, Mr. Ainslee, Collector of Customs at Quebec, reported to the Board, Canadian exports of wheat, flour and biscuit. (B.T. 5/1, fol. 45.)

	Wheat. bushels.	*Flour. bushels.*	*Biscuit. quintals.*
1770	51,800	1400	—
1771	193,800	823	—
1772	233,300	1430	—
1773	264,900	2380	—
1774	460,800	1300	4000
1775	175,000	2500	4600
1776	56,000	1060	1200
1777	17,000	7900	4000

" From this last period," concludes his evidence, " a Prohibition upon the export of wheat and flour and all species of provisions took place by Proclamation, with a view to assure a supply for the army." Whitehall, March 18, 1784.

Ainslee's statistics reveal the transfer of food products to troops outside

work and build and repair fortifications. As a result, hardly two years had elapsed before the province began to experience the pangs of serious scarcity.

On October 25, 1776, the British Government laid a general embargo on the export of provisions from Great Britain and Ireland with a view to the scarcity of seamen for transport as well as the need for conserving food. This was continued with certain relaxations until the end of the war.[1] Forced to rely largely on his own efforts, Governor Haldimand found it necessary in May, 1777, to prohibit by proclamation the exportation of all live stock, and of corn, flour and biscuits until the arrival of the victualling ships.[2] In October, improved prospects induced him to lift the restriction,[3] and during the year 1778, Newfoundland and Nova Scotia were fairly well supplied. But early in the following year an attempt was made by certain war profiteers to " corner " all the wheat and flour in the province. To a degree, they were successful, and prices rose to an exorbitant height.[4] At Quebec, wheat sold for $2.00 a bushel, and flour for $8.00 a cwt. At one time a renewal of the old punitive legislation against " persons who shall be deemed Forestallers, Regraters and Ingrossers " was considered.[5] But on this occasion Haldimand felt that a renewal of the prohibition forbidding export would be sufficient in itself with less danger of discouraging cultivation.[6] A proclamation to this effect was successful in reducing prices within reason[7] and Providence in the form of a tolerably good season's crop gave final confirmation to legislative decree.

the colony and to Nova Scotia and Newfoundland ; but they fail to show the huge importations of food from England into Canada, to make good the deficit.

[1] As in the case of arms, some relaxations were permitted. Before the end of 1780, about 680 passes were granted to provision ships for the colonies, 350 to the West Indies, 165 to New York, 44 to Newfoundland and 60 to Canada, Nova Scotia and Hudson's Bay. See *Acts of the Privy Council, Colonial*, Vol. V, p. 446.

[2] Proclamation of May 9, 1777, C.O. 42/36.

[3] Proclamation of October 11, 1777, C.O. 45/3.

[4] Haldimand to the Secretary of State, Oct. 25, 1780, C.O. 43/14, fol. 305.

[5] *Acts of the Privy Council, Colonial*, Vol. V, p. 507–8.

[6] *Ibid.* The Board of Trade sanctioned the prohibitory ordinance, but expressed itself against any " punishment clauses." *Journal of the Board of Trade*, April 3, 1781, C.O. 391/88, fol. 186.

[7] *Acts of Privy Council, Colonial*, Vol. VI, p. 582. Regarding this food shortage, see Haldimand to Germaine, Sept. 13, 1779, C.O. 43/14, fol. 171 ; also Bryan Edwards, *op. cit.*, II, p. 403.

By 1780, this prohibition was definitely established in the form of an Ordinance, which remained in force until the end of the war.[1] Lord George Germaine was able to appreciate Haldimand's foresight and caution. In the following July, he complimented the governor on having "found means to subsist the troops without subjecting the public to the exactions of interested individuals."[2]

Yet the main justification for Haldimand's policy of caution lay in the astonishing collapse of the British Navy. American privateers swept the seas, and before the entrance of France into the war, almost a thousand British trading vessels were lost by capture. After 1778, the annual average of losses rose to nearly 600 ships; and before the war ended, almost exactly 3000 British merchantmen had fallen into the hands of the enemy.[3] Provision ships waited months for convoys or sailed alone at risk of capture.[4] Early in the summer of 1780, the Quebec victualling fleet of fifteen ships fell victim to pestering enemy frigates off the coast of Newfoundland, and similar mishaps continued to add to the already heavy burden of the Canadian governor.[5] All Haldimand's letters during this period exhibit a painful anxiety which the desultory movements of

[1] Ordinance of March 9, 1780, 20 Geo. III, cap. I: "To prohibit for a limited time, the exportation of wheat, peas, oats, biscuit, flour or meal of any kind; also of horned cattle; and thereby to reduce the present high price of wheat and flour." C.O. 44/3.

[2] McIlwraith, Jean, *Life of General Haldimand* (Makers of Canada), p. 178. The British forces in Canada annually consumed on an average 12,000 bushels of flour, and 6000 bushels of biscuit; see *Acts of Privy Council, Col.*, Vol. VI, p. 581.

According to the evidence of Mr. Atkinson before the Board of Trade, "During the late war the army in Canada amounted to no more than 15,000 men, and the colony could not provide for them. *The whole supply was sent from England. Relying for one year on the colony, the army nearly starved.*" "*Canada,*" he concluded, "*was almost in the same state of cultivation as in 1760.*" *Board of Trade Mins.*, B.T. 5/1, fols. 14–15.

[3] Sir G. O. Trevelyan, *Geo. III and Chas. James Fox*, Vol. V, p. 158; Laird Clowes, W., *The Royal Navy*, Vol. III, p. 396. For a list of vessels foundered, wrecked, etc., see Vol. IV, p. 109. Note also *Parl. Hist.*, XIX, pp. 709–12, *passim.*

[4] See Petition of merchants of London trading to Quebec, as considered by Lord George Germaine and Lords Commissioners of Admiralty, London, Feb. 13, 1781, C.O. 42/41.

[5] Quebec was rarely self-sufficient during the war. To prevent fluctuation of the import and export of grain, Gov. Pownall's Act (13 Geo. III, c. 43) was enforced, and whenever the price of wheat fell below 5*s*. 6*d*. per bushel the importation was stopped; if lower, a bounty of 5*s*. per quarter on export was paid until it again advanced. Anderson, *History of Commerce,* IV, pp. 303, 398.

the yearly supply ships occasioned. There was never much grain in the country, and troops "pinched for food" were billeted over the entire province.[1] Petition upon petition appeared before the Board of Trade and the Admiralty, pointing out the loss from delays and from lack of protection. In fact, the greater part of the Board of Trade's business during this period concerns consideration of these pleas for special licences to import provisions as well as arms and ammunition in the interest of the province and the Indian trade.[2]

And yet when merchants suffering from an accumulation of heavy financial losses rose up in wrath, the administration replied that "the Navy was the sure shield of defence." The Commons derived little comfort from that statement. When Edmund Burke, wearied of the disclosures of incompetence provided by the Navy debate, hurled the Book of Estimates at the Treasury Bench,[3] he was merely giving active expression to an indignation which infected the whole House.

The Admiralty under the presidency of the notorious Lord Sandwich was subjected to increasingly damaging attacks. More money had been granted on the extraordinary estimate alone, "than would have built from the stocks rigged and completely equipped for sea 100 men of war," yet at the moment the whole navy had only about thirty-five ships of the line fit for sea.[4] The protection of sea-borne commerce was inadequate; there were not enough frigates; ships were rotting to pieces and foundering owing to inferior foreign timber; money for repairs was being wasted in jobbery and corruption.[5]

[1] In a letter of Sept. 13, 1779, he remarks, "From what I have said in relation to the state of the grain in this country, your Lordship will see how very fortunate it was for the King's service and indeed for the People, that a Resolution was taken of sending English flour to this province." He mentions that of 13 victuallers sailing from Cork, on April 30 last, only 10 arrived. C.O. 43/14, fol. 171.

[2] See Minutes of the Board of Trade for the period 1773–82, C.O. 388, ff. 59–74. For the export of arms and ammunition, only about 350 passes were granted, of which 80 went to Quebec, about 40 to the Floridas and 150 to the West Indies; *Acts of the Privy Council, Colonial*, Vol. V, p. 401.

[3] Debate on the Naval Estimates, Feb. 13, 1777; *Parl. Hist.*, XIX, p. 729.

[4] *Ibid.*, pp. 728–30, 818–34, 874–95; XX, 204–38, 372. See also, Wraxall, *Historical Memoirs*, p. 498.

[5] See Middleton to Sandwich, 1779, describing the lamentable state of the fleet. "Unless a new plan is adopted and your lordship gives your whole time to the business of the Admiralty, the misapplication of the fleet will bring ruin upon this country." *Letters and Papers of Charles, Lord Barham*. Edited by Sir John Knox Laughton, Vol. II, p. 3.

In his recently published *Correspondence of King George III*, Sir John Fortescue has done little to erase Sandwich's record of corruption; but he has supplied materials which go far to show that the feebleness of the British Navy could by no means be laid entirely at the door of Admiralty misgovernment. "We have no friend or ally to assist us," said Sandwich, "on the contrary all those who ought to be our allies except Portugal, act against us in supplying our enemies with the means of equipping their fleets."[1] England was cut off from her usual foreign sources of naval stores, and drawing on her own small reserves for tar, pitch, oak planks, masts, deal and spars.[2] Added to this, the exigencies of the war left no time for proper timber seasoning.[3] In consequence it was estimated that by April, 1780, there would only be about fifty ships fit for sea, and many of these cripples.[4] Before that date arrived, Florida was the only province south of Canada which remained to the Crown.[5]

[1] "Thoughts upon Naval measures to be taken Sept. 14, 1779, with an account of the then State of the English Fleet." Fortescue, *Correspondence of Geo. III*, Vol. IV, p. 441, No. 2776.

[2] See Wooldridge's testimony to the Lords, for the effect of the war on the price and scarcity of naval stores, *Parliamentary History*, XIX, p. 709; also note, "Answers to Enquiries of the Secretary of State," by the Lieutenant-Governor of Jamaica, Nov. 11, 1784, C.O. 137, 85.

[3] *Sandwich's Defence of His Administration of the Navy*, Fortescue, Vol. V, 342, 351.

[4] *Ibid.*, Vol. IV, p. 439. Sir Chas. Hardy's Fleet, 40; nearly ready for sea, 6; coming from West Indies, 8; in shipwrights' hands, 4.

[5] Admiral of the Fleet Sir Thomas Byam Martin, summed up the situation at the end of the war with candid deliberation. "It may easily be imagined, that five years of such demand upon the naval resources of the country was very exhausting, and it appears by official documents that when the ships were paid off in the termination of the war in 1783, they were in a wretched state of feebleness and decay, insomuch that there was not a sound ship in the fleet. Several returning home had foundered on the Banks of Newfoundland owing to their ill-construction and rickety condition." *Letters and Papers of Admiral of the Fleet Sir Thomas Byam Martin*; Edited by Sir R. V. Hamilton, Vol. III, p. 379.

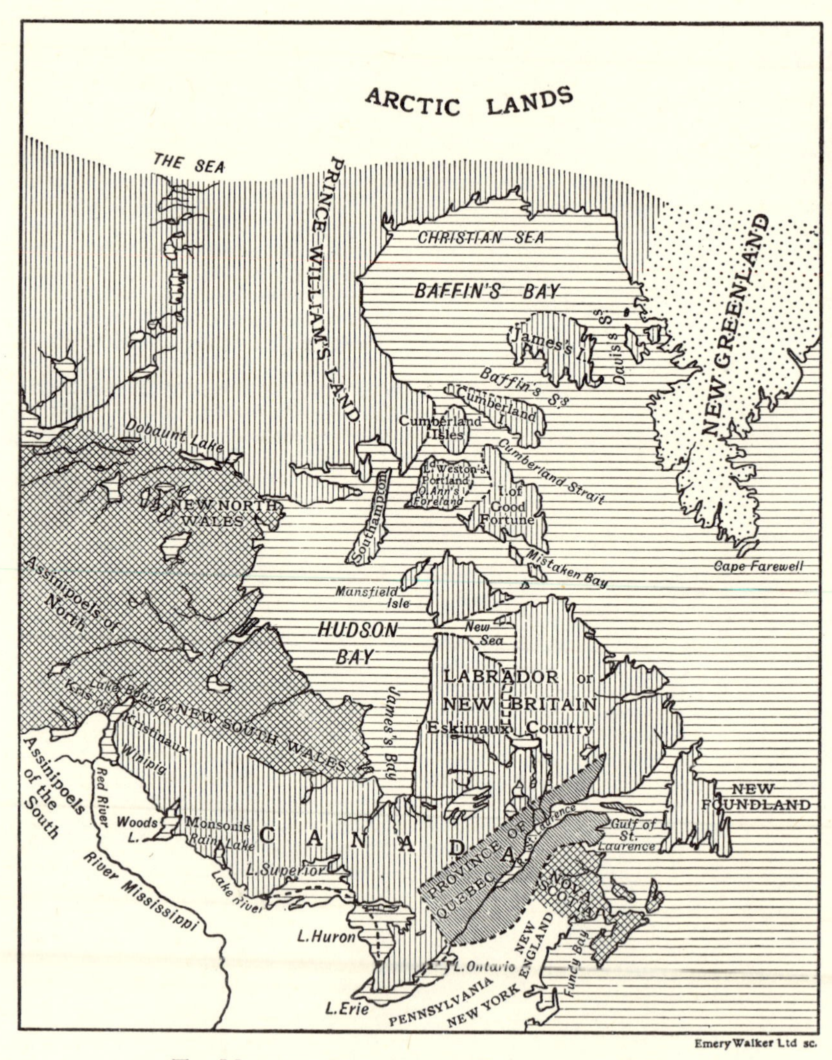

THE MISSISSIPI RIVER AND THE BOUNDARY OF 1783.

(*From a Map published by J. Wilkes, London, May 20th,* 1797.)

CHAPTER IV

THE SETTLEMENT OF 1783

THE Treaty of Versailles, following twenty years after the memorable acquisition of Canada in 1763, provides a further opportunity for studying the status of the northern colony in the Old Colonial System. On this second occasion the negotiations were not affected by *quid pro quo* balancings of territory. Canada had been preserved from conquest and it became largely a question of how much of the country was worth retaining, in order to guarantee a lasting peace with the security of a reasonable share of British North American trade. Territory in terms of square miles and raw products was to be weighed in the balance against the accumulating influence of an aggressive free trade group who voiced the new economic liberalism of Adam Smith.

Franklin expressed one great ideal of the British negotiators in a paper which he permitted the commissioner, Oswald, to carry to the Prime Minister, Lord Shelburne[1]—" To make a peace durable, what may give occasion for future wars should if practicable be removed."[2] But Franklin's solution of the problem was hardly so acceptable.[3] " Britain possesses Canada. Her chief advantage from that possession consists in the trade for peltry. Her expenses in governing and defending that settlement must be considerable. It might be humiliating to her to give it up on the demand of America. Perhaps America will not demand it ; some of her political rulers may consider the fear of such a neighbour as the means of keeping the thirteen states more united among themselves and more attentive to military discipline. But on the mind of the

[1] Rockingham died on July 1, and his death brought the division of the Whigs to a head. Fox and his party, Portland, Cavendish, Burke and Sheridan resigned, and a new ministry was formed under Shelburne.

[2] Lord Fitzmaurice, *Life of the Earl of Shelburne*, Vol. II, p. 119.

[3] Franklin's *Journal*, July 1, 1782 ; in Wharton, *Diplomatic Correspondence of the American Revolution*, Vol. V, p. 541.

people in general, would it not have an excellent effect if Britain should voluntarily offer to give up this province, though on these conditions, that *she shall in all times coming have and enjoy the right of free trade thither unencumbered with any duties whatsoever.*"

Oswald evidently entertained this idea[1]; but it is more than doubtful if Lord Shelburne ever gave serious consideration to the proposition. The Prime Minister was fully aware how Parliament would receive a treaty which wiped out the whole of the British fur trade on the American continent. Nevertheless, it is apparent throughout the conference that Franklin had unshaken confidence in his country's ability to obtain from Great Britain all she asked and probably more.[2] From all evidence, he seems to have believed that his colleagues might well have insisted upon the cession of Canada, if they had urged their claims as strenuously as they did the American right to the Newfoundland fisheries, and had satisfied the demands made on behalf of the loyalists.[3]

This attitude on the part of the American negotiators revealed a fair understanding of the general intentions of British diplomacy. Over and above differences in temperament and personality between British Secretaries of State and their delegates, one objective stood paramount—reconciliation and "rights of trade," and the American envoys never failed to appreciate that point of view. They encouraged the rampant prejudice against colonies which sooner or later dropped off in the manner of Turgot's "ripe fruit." If the true interests of British imperialism lay in the development of trade and commerce, why bother about vast tracts of wilderness, which

[1] Franklin reports in his *Journal* for July 1, 1782, that "Oswald said he had told the ministers before he came away that he thought no recompense to those people [Loyalists] was to be expected from us; that he had also in consequence of our former conversation on the subject, given it as his opinion that Canada should be given up to the U.S., as it would prevent the occasion of future difference; and *as the government of such a country was worth nothing, and of no importance if they could have the free commerce,* that the Marquis of Rockingham and Lord Shelburne, though they spoke reservedly, did not seem very averse to it, but that Mr. Fox appeared to be startled at the proposition. He was, however, not without hopes that it would be agreed to." Wharton, *op. cit.*, V, pp. 571–2.

[2] See Alvord, C. W., *Lord Shelburne and the Founding of British-American Goodwill.* The Raleigh Lecture in History to the British Academy, London, 1918.

[3] See Lecky, *History of England*, Vol. V, Chap. XV, p. 153; and Perkins, J.B., *France in the American Revolution*, p. 484.

involved huge expense, and brought profits only to a limited group of merchant fur traders. If England were given adequate commercial privileges in North America, " in all times coming, to have and enjoy the right of free trade thither, unencumbered with any duties whatsoever," the cession of Canada would be no loss, and even a net gain. On the other hand, if Canada were to be preserved, for the same reasons, the matter of a southern boundary was of no special significance.

John Jay stated the case concisely in a letter to Livingstone.[1] " It was impolitic for Britain to oppose America on the point of boundary because the profits of an extensive and lucrative commerce, and not the possession of vast tracts of wilderness were the true objects of a commercial nation. By extending to the Mississippi on the West, and to the ' proclamation bounds ' of Canada on the north, and by permitting mutually free navigation of the lakes and rivers, there would be an inland navigation from the Gulf of St. Lawrence to the Gulf of Mexico. By such means, the inhabitants west and north of the mountains could be more easily supplied with foreign commodities than from the ports on the Atlantic. This immense and growing trade could be monopolised by Great Britain, since America would not insist that other nations be admitted to navigate her waters. It was therefore not wise for Britain to think of extending Canada southward or retaining any part of a country which was not in her power to settle and govern."

Shelburne's attitude in response to this diplomatic effort, is best expressed by Thomas Pownall. Early in 1782, he defined his conception of the aims of British policy in *A Memorial in Two Parts*,[2] which proved in many ways to be a repetition of Shelburne's own views as contained in the prophetic speech of 1762. But Pownall was not the leader of a party and a government. He was able to state his opinions without the mufflers of political expediency which sometimes stifled Shelburne during this period.

Between 1757 and 1760, he had been successively Governor

[1] Letter of November 17, 1782; Wharton, *op. cit.*, Vol. VI, p. 31.

[2] *A Memorial in Two Parts*, originally intended to be presented to the King, with explanatory Preface (completed Jan. 2, 1782), Part II, pp. 34–35.

of Massachusetts and South Carolina, and he was one of the best informed men in England on colonial affairs. His views with regard to the connection were much the same as those of Pitt, and his scheme of imperial federation may quite possibly have been the basis of Pitt's own proposals in 1777.[1] Pownall maintained that the possession of Quebec and Nova Scotia was highly necessary so long as Great Britain retained her plantations in the West Indies—" they were sources from whence (at a certainty under all events) these islands could draw their necessary supply of lumber, fish and livestock." They were also vitally necessary to Britain as a naval power. Without them she could have no naval station, command or protection in the American seas. With them she might have all these, although they might not be able to supply at present her navy with all the naval stores that she might want. They would, however, supply sufficient to ward off the monopoly which some of the northern powers of Europe had formerly endeavoured to establish against Britain, and might again as far as such could be established, use it hostilely against her.

He then went on to describe Canada's value as a strategic base for trade. Even though her own potentialities might not be vast, she could perform most useful service as Gate and Highway for the trade further south. " The province of Quebec had control of the supply and of the market not only of the Indians, but of all the inhabitants of the back countries. By reason of the easy water communications, British goods could be marketed more cheaply than any other—and the custom of those territories would be a matter of course."

Pownall's point of view was the accepted view of the British negotiators, and it did contain a basis for compromise through concession. British ambitions for an enlarged sphere of commerce should be reconciled to the American demands for expansion ; boundaries should be sacrificed for trade privileges.

But there was one great obstacle in the way. Such a negotiation implied a trade agreement with an alien country, and this

[1] Pownall's views on colonial policy are ably expressed in his *Administration of Colonies*. The 4th edition of this work, 1768, contains a dedication to George Grenville, urging the attachment of the colonies to the Mother Country, but with a limitation as to taxation. The British Isles, he declared, " were a grand marine dominion," and ought to be united into " one imperium in one centre where the seat of government is." P. XV.

involved a modification of the sacred navigation laws. To effect such an adjustment would have been a formidable task for a dictator. In this instance, a man holding the precarious post of Prime Minister under George III, was prepared to carry it out. At an early period in his life, Lord Shelburne had come under the influence of Adam Smith and had become a convert to free trade. Like Chatham he had been reluctant to concede independence;[1] but finally, reconciled to the idea, he was anxious to retain America within the commercial fold on the basis of the new and daring principle of economic advantage—freedom of trade.

On October 8, 1782, certain articles were agreed to by the American and British commissioners and sent to England for the king's consideration.[2] Article 4 specifically carried into effect Shelburne's policy of permanent peace and continued commercial intercourse. It declared that the "navigation of the River Mississippi from its source to the ocean shall forever remain free and open, and that both there, and in all rivers, harbours, lakes, ports and places belonging to his Britannic Majesty or to the United States, or in any part of the world, the merchant ships of the one and the other shall be received, treated and protected like the merchant ships of the sovereign country." In other words, American shipping would enjoy the same privileges, and be liable to the same charges and duties as British shipping.

The inclusion of this article in the Preliminaries would have more than anticipated Jay's Treaty. But the time was not ripe. Although Adam Smith might be laureated, banqueted and lionized by Society, he was not seriously accepted by the majority of Englishmen.[3] The Ministry avoided the issue. At their wish alone, it was resolved to leave commercial

[1] Shelburne to the King, Sept. 15, 1782: "As to the general measure, I am as clearly of opinion against a Peace as I ever was against American independence, till in fact the Resolutions of the House of Commons decided the point." Fortescue, *op. cit.*, Vol. VI, p. 128.

[2] Wharton, *op. cit.*, Vol. V, p. 805.

[3] The famous German economist, George Sartorius, in his review of the *Wealth of Nations* (1793), remarked, "A work that requires so much effort and thought will at first find little sale. The faith in old principles which are to be found in so many compendia is so mild and sweet, and thinking and comprehending a new darkly worded doctrine requires so much time and effort. . . ." *Göttingische Gelehrte Anzeigen*, Art. 19, pp. 1661–2 (1793).

arrangements to a separate treaty, and this meant indefinite postponement.

According to Franklin, the reason given by the British negotiators for dropping the clause relating to commerce was the fact that "some statutes were in the way which must be repealed before a treaty of that kind could be well formed, and this was a matter to be considered in Parliament."[1] This explanation may have been technically true. Yet, the precipitate withdrawal of Article IV shows only too clearly the tenacious hold of mercantilist principles on English political life. Shelburne in 1782 and Pitt in the following year were a generation ahead of their time, and helpless to apply their new-born wisdom. No tampering economists might violate the sanctity of Navigation Laws.

The whole transaction does, however, exhibit the vital importance of one aspect of British policy. It is obvious from the emphasis which was laid on the freedom of the Mississippi, that the particular trade of the back country loomed up as much more important than the interests of sundry British-Canadian fur merchants in the region of the St. Lawrence and Ohio. An appreciation of this fact, as fundamental to the general policy of permanent peace and "rights of trade" makes more intelligible the sacrifice of Canadian boundaries.

The Canadian frontier had always been in doubt, even after it had been generally settled by the Quebec Act of 1774. The new treaty, the preliminaries of which were signed on November 30, 1782, gave it real definition. It was decided to abandon the line which had included the Ohio country, as well as the boundary of 1754, when it belonged to the French; and to take a new and intermediate boundary extending through the Great Lakes. This allowed to the United States the huge section called the Old North West, between the Alleghanies and the Mississippi, a country equal in area to one third of Europe and representing an immense fur trading preserve, which the Quebec Act had assessed as belonging to Canada.

When these surprising preliminaries were made public, the New York Coffee House hummed with the angry activity of

[1] Franklin to Livingston, Passy, Dec. 5, 1782. Wharton, VI, 113.

a hive of bees. In this, their London headquarters, the alarmed Canada merchants assembled in the early days of 1783, and drew up a memorial of protest, which they addressed to Lord Shelburne.[1] They pointed out that the line according to the second provisional article would strike the River St. Lawrence about fifty miles above Montreal, a fact rather inconsistent with the security of what remained of Canada ; that it cut off Fort Oswegatchie, Fort Carleton Island, Fort Oswego, Fort Niagara with its important carrying place and the small fort of Little Niagara, Fort Detroit, Fort Michilimackinac and the carrying place of St. Mary's. From Lake Superior, it travelled north of the vital Grand Portage, the only communication with the extensive country to the north-west ; then, proceeding to the north-west point of the Lake of the Woods and from thence westwards to the Mississippi, which it was supposed to cross, it cut off all the trading posts and about twenty-five Indian tribes, the trade with whom was the grand object of the commercial intercourse between Great Britain and the province of Quebec.

Furthermore, the new boundary did not include Lake Michigan. The importance of this waterway in the Great Lakes chain has often been under-estimated. John Conolly, a merchant of substance and intelligence, wrote privately to Lord Shelburne, and declared it to be the gravest loss of all, " of more consequence in the Indian trade than all the others collectively."[2] Conolly was thinking in terms of Mississippi trade. The navigation of that river was allowed, but, as he and the merchants were able to show, the river was not navigable as far as Canada, and even if it were, no liberty had been given for landing goods on the Spanish or American sides, nor protection for the traders.[3]

Conolly, evidently with certain merchant support, urged an amendment, advocating a line from the western extremity of Lake Erie to Lake Michigan. " By this means, the navigation of the Mississippi would be valuable to Great Britain ; which otherwise appears as an article unnecessary to have

[1] Canada Merchants to Shelburne, Jan. 31, 1783, Shelburne MS., Vol. 72, f. 83.
[2] Feb. 1, 1783, Shelburne MS., Vol. 72, f. 79.
[3] *Ibid.*, Vol. 72, f. 83.

been inserted in the Treaty of accommodation; and by this measure it will be in our power to come in for, not only a fair division of the trade, but it will put us also upon a more equitable footing with the Americans, who are at liberty to supply themselves by the River St. Lawrence should the Mississippi on any occasion appear less eligible." "If your Lordship could obtain so valuable an acquisition . . . the British manufactures will have a free and uncontrolled entrance into the Illinois country, and may stand in competition with commodities of the same nature imported from France at the trading posts; and as our merchants have in general better capitals than most other commercial people, 'tis reasonable to suppose that we should ultimately gain the ascendancy and that the American trader would find his interest in purchasing from us rather than elsewhere, especially when avenues to the Indian commerce are open to both people. . . ."[1]

The Ministry made no admission of their geographical miscalculation with regard to the source of the Mississippi. On February 6, Oswald met a committee of the Canada merchants and informed them that it was the "real intention and spirit of the Treaty" that a free participation of "all the Lakes, Rivers and carrying places" should be enjoyed by all British subjects on the same terms and conditions as those of American States.[2] This, indeed, would have been a fact had Article IV of the October preliminaries been retained; but the discarding of that provision for a commerce mutually free from restriction rendered Oswald's statement literally untrue.

In Parliament as in the New York Coffee House, the Treaty became the subject of heated attack and controversy. The powerful Opposition thundered against the desertion of the Loyalists, the granting away of the Fisheries,[3] and the running

[1] Shelburne MS., Vol. 72, f. 79.

[2] Memorandum contained in Chatham MSS., Bundle 343; also quoted by the Canada merchants in their memorial to Shelburne of Feb. 6, 1783, C.O. 5/8.

[3] The third article of the Provisionals was a triumph for New England diplomacy, and represents an almost unbelievable submission. The Americans claiming the same rights as the French, who held St. Pierre and Miquellon, were permitted to fish on all the cherished banks of Newfoundland and in the Gulf of St. Lawrence, although they were forbidden to dry or cure fish on the island of Newfoundland. But, as was rather bitterly remarked by English merchants, there was no corresponding authorisation for British subjects to

of a boundary line through the Great Lakes with the loss of the Old North West.[1] In the House of Lords, Carlisle declared, " You had better have ceded all Canada than given in to this mockery of keeping the two ports of Montreal and Quebec (for they are no other than mere ports) without the trade of their interior country."[2] From the other side of the ocean, Governor Haldimand wrote to Lord North that, without the fur posts, Canada was worth little. " It will be a matter of great doubt whether it would be right to spend much money for the preservation of it, or at least it would never be worth while to go to war about it."[3] Germaine, now breathing the freer air of opposition, wrote to Knox—" was it ignorance or treachery that induced the late Ministers to act as they did in whatever related to the commercial interest of this country ? Lord Shelburne plainly intended it should be given up, or he would not have permitted Oswald to settle such a boundary."[4]

If Shelburne were to be judged by his speech in defence of the Treaty before the Lords, he would certainly not be recognizable as Shelburne, the bold imperialist of 1762. His reply in that House resounded gloomily, like an admission of failure.[5] He emphasized the low state of the country, a result

fish on American coasts. The concession, however, provides another indication of the American envoy's recognition of the trend of British policy during the negotiations. John Adams, to whom credit for this diplomatic success is chiefly due, contended that if the Americans were excluded from the fisheries they would not be able to carry fish to Spain and Portugal, and with the proceeds of their sales to buy commodities in England.

[1] " *It is dangerous to base convictions about possible policy upon the speeches of men in opposition*. Still, from what was said then, and from other sources of information, it seems evident that if North or Portland or Fox had been the responsible minister, the Old North West would probably *not* have been ceded to the United States ; and, if finally, it would have been only after a bitter struggle." Alvord, C. W., *Lord Shelburne and the Founding of British-American Goodwill*, p. 19.

[2] *Parl. History*, Vol. XXIII, p. 377, Feb. 17, 1783.

[3] Haldimand to North, Oct. 27, 1783, C.O. 42/46.

[4] Sackville to Knox, July 4, 1783, in Knox, *Extra-Official State Papers*, App. ii, XVII. A curious reflection of this same feeling is contained in a letter, which the Rev. Chas. Morgan enclosed and sent to Nepean. It was posted from New York, dated Jan. 3, 1786, and signed Aug. V. Horne. After referring to Loyalist migrations, which he was assisting, the letter continues, " This measure you know I should have adopted the moment peace was declared, but for an apprehension (and, in which I was not singular) that Great Britain from the strange and unaccountable Division of that country intended not long to be burthened with Canada." Morgan to Nepean, March 10, 1786, C.O. 42/87.

[5] *Parl. History*, Vol. XXIII, p. 409. See also, *Reflections on the Preliminary and Provisional Articles*, London, 1783, and *Observations on the Preliminary and Provisional Articles*, London, 1783.

of the blunderings of former ministers, now in opposition. The Treasury was empty, the Army defeated and the Navy in decay. Furthermore, Fox's premature statement of the Government's intentions to proclaim Independence had handicapped the negotiators in their bargaining with France and Spain. But even if compulsion had affected so extensive a boundary line, now that peace had been established, was the loss of any great moment ? The military protection of Canada had cost far more than the trade was worth, and the monopolistic ambitions of a few merchants must not be allowed to interfere with a wider imperial policy. The total annual value of the fur trade was no more than £50,000,[1] and at present Canada was costing the Government a million pounds per annum.

But it was not the true Shelburne who spoke in the Lords' debate. The idealist who had drawn glowing pictures of a future Canada during the negotiations of 1763, drew a curtain of gloom in Parliament to veil the scene of '83. Fortunately, however, we have a transcription of Shelburne's truer, finer sentiments following the event. Some time in 1783, there was published a small volume entitled *Considerations on the Provisional Articles.*[2] The author was Andrew Kippis, but the fount of his knowledge was Lord Shelburne.

On the whole question concerning the Canada boundaries, the Government, declared the writer, held two views, the one political, the other commercial. With regard to the first, " it was certainly prescribed that we should lay the foundation of another large and liberal system, the first object of which should be permanent peace. To the attainment of this end it was necessary to prevent every ground of future jealousies and quarrels." The next consideration, the commercial, supplied the root explanation of Shelburne's diplomacy during

[1] Shelburne Abstracts, Feb., 1783, (Brit. Mus.), Add. MS. 24131. This remark was a gross untruth, of which Shelburne must surely have been aware. In 1780, the trade to the Upper Countries was reported to be worth £200,000 sterling. See *Can. Archives Report*, 1888, Note E, p. 59. In 1785 Lt.-Gov. Hamilton reported the trade to be worth £180,000, of which £100,000 came from within the limits of the United States. (*C.A. Report*, 1890, Note C, p. 56). See also McLaughlin, A. C, " Western Posts and British Debts," *Annual Report Am. Historical Assoc.*, 1894, and Stevens, W. E., *The North West Fur Trade, 1763–1800* (University of Illinois Studies in the Social Sciences), Vol. XIV, No. 3, Sept., 1926.

[2] *Considerations on the Provisional Articles*, p. 42.

the negotiations. "It was necessary to proceed upon the establishment of a new principle, a principle which hath already notoriously taken place in the instance of Ireland, and which is avowed by America, not only to England, but to all the powers of Europe. *The system of monopolies and little restrictions in trade begins to be exploded in the world, and will justly every day grow more and more out of fashion. It is for the real honour of Great Britain to prosecute an enlarged plan of commerce,* and to have contended about a few furs would have been incompatible with a design of such magnitude and importance."

The disciple of Adam Smith was interpreting the pressing demands of the Industrial Revolution in the light of the new bible of political economy, *The Wealth of Nations.* It represented the first attempt to translate the principle of free trade into British policy. A new sort of idealism had crept into English political life, an idealism which was prepared to sacrifice territorial prestige to the grander project of "an enlarged plan of commerce," on a continental scale. But in many ways it was a concept fraught with danger, for its attainment in the form of an applied policy depended on the Cobden assumption, that other nations would accept the same principle of conduct in return. For that period, success was assured only because a new born nation was dependent on the British manufacturer for its development and expansion. Even then, Shelburne had risked the whole north-west fur trade and had jeopardized the very existence of Canada on the altruistic hope that America would enter permanently into a project of commercial freedom.

Nevertheless, Shelburne may claim to be the first statesman who took a firm and active stand against the oligarchic powers of monopoly, which hitherto had dominated British policy. In wise generalship, as a diplomatist, he had perhaps, failed; but the mantle of Liberal imperialism which he had received from Adam Smith was to be handed onward to the Younger Pitt.

Adam Smith had remarked that the expectation of a rupture with the colonies had struck the people of England with more terror than they had ever felt for a Spanish Armada or a French invasion.[1] Now that the rupture had occurred, they

[1] *Wealth of Nations* (ed. E. Cannan), Vol. II, p. 105.

did not realize what cataclysmic change had automatically been wrought in their own colonial system, and continued dismally to estimate the effects of revolution on the basis of old theory. Shelburne, before he had become reconciled to dissolution, surpassed even Chatham in expressions of despair. Many times, he had declared to the Lords that " the Sun of England's glory was set for ever,"[1] although at a later stage he admitted it was his resolution to " improve the twilight." Germaine, in the Commons, had maintained, as a position admitting of no doubt, that " from the instant when American independence should be acknowledged the British Empire was ruined."[2]

And by all the old canons of mercantilist theory, England was ruined. As Adam Smith details at length, she had sacrificed her European for her colonial trade. The Treaty of Paris had destroyed the colonial monopoly, on which she had come to depend for her prosperity; and now the House of Commons was confronted with the question, "Can you expect a mighty giant to shrivel himself up into a dwarf?"[3]

With the exception of that congenial " œconomist " circle, Tucker, Price, Priestley and Hume, as well as Adam Smith and one or two others, the politicians of the country and of the Continent believed that the independence of the colonies had decided the fate of England. Some years after, Dean Tucker satirized the popular opinion of the day. " Nay, those patriotic worthies, the news writers, not only proclaimed the Downfall of the Commerce of this opulent kingdom, but also ventured to foretell that a set of Ciceronis would appear in a century or two, who were to conduct inquisitive strangers over the ruins of this our once great Metropolis. ' Here, Gentlemen, stood Westminster Hall and adjoining to it was the Parliament House. Let us now go and view another famous ruin. Here, Gentlemen, was a place called the Royal Exchange, where merchants used to meet, when merchants used to live.' "[4]

[1] One occasion was during his gloomy peroration of July 10, 1782, as referred to above. See Wraxall, *Memoirs*, p. 515, also *Parl. History*, XXIII, p. 194.

[2] Wraxall, *op. cit.*, p. 515.

[3] Roscher, Wilhelm, *Kolonien*, etc., p. 223; Huskisson, W., *Edinburgh Review*, Vol. 42.

[4] Perhaps this was the original of Lord Macaulay's New Zealander.

Among the " œconomists " and a good many of the Rockingham Whigs, there was a feeling of relief rather than regret, judging by the debates in Parliament. In fact, some Whigs now began to pride themselves upon having asserted the futility of the late scheme of Empire from the first,[1] and argued that emigration and imperial wars would both impoverish a country.[2] And there were those foolhardy ones who were willing to maintain with the essayist that separation is not real " unless we continue to alienate their affection and the natural channel of their trade." Since there is no longer the expense of administration, " the dismemberment of America is rather a gain than a loss to us ; and if we maintain a superior navy to the rest of Europe and America, we may bid defiance to the combined world either to annoy our countries or injure our commerce."[3]

The miracle the essayist foretold came true. Because England through the progressing Industrial Revolution could produce better and more cheaply than any other nation, the United States continued to be her best customer, and bought more, not less than under the old system of monopoly. The volume of trade doubled in fifteen years after the treaty, and Adam Smith's doctrines were vindicated, though they were not generally believed.[4]

[1] Bigelow, J., *Franklin*, iii, p. 86, and *Consolatory Thoughts on American Independence*, 1782, pp. 3, 11.

[2] " In regard to Population," says the Dean of Gloucester, " it is to be feared that our numbers have not increased, nay, they have decreased since the year 1759 . . . ; the emigrations from Great Britain and Ireland since the *fatal acquisition of Canada* have been enormous, and almost incredible, so that were I to say that *6000 persons* have emigrated annually at an average to North America from these two islands, I should be greatly within the mark." *The State of the Nation in 1777 compared with the State of the Nation in the famous year of Conquest and of Glory, 1759*. (Brit. Mus.) Add. MS. 34414, fol. 568.

[3] *Essay* [on] *the True Interests and Resources of the Empire of Great Britain and Ireland*, etc., by the Earl of A——L. Dublin, 1783. (Brit. Mus.)

[4] See *Parl. History*, Vol. XXV, p. 1372. In the debate in the Commons on the Bill for the Encouragement of Shipping and Navigation, Jenkinson remarked on the astonishing increase of shipping after 1784, " from 94,000 tons of freightage to 110,000."

Dean Tucker declared that " the Trade of Great Britain rests on a much firmer foundation than that of a normal subjection by means of Paper Laws and imaginary restrictions. A Foundation so very obvious as well as secure, that it is surprising it hath not been taken notice of in this dispute. The Foundation I mean is the superiority of the British Capitals over those of every other country in the Universe. . . ." This reference to the power of " long credits " in securing American trade was emphasized by Lord Sheffield in

Yet a steady adhesion to old ways of thought was in some ways inevitable. The policy of "triple monopoly" as embodied in the Trade and Navigation Laws had been growing to maturity ever since 1650, and its principles had been closely knit into the national life. Furthermore "big interests" had been created—shipowners, sugar planters and certain classes of merchants—whose prosperity depended on the continuance of the system. Indeed, many Englishmen continued to place the application of the mercantile system so far in the front rank of policy that Lord Sheffield could say in 1784, that "the only use of the American colonies or West India Islands is the monopoly of their consumption and the carriage of their produce."[1]

Canada's position remained, therefore, one of direct subordination to the commercial development of the Mother Country. But two great facts, a spreading industrialism which emphasized more strongly than ever the need for increased markets and a disastrous war which pointed to serious naval deficiencies, were giving that development a new and vigorous turn. Sheffield had linked colonial supply and the carrying trade, as representing the standard of colonial utility. A new generation was to declare that "the grand motive for the acquisition of colonies" was "the increase of our merchant shipping," and secondly, "the vending of our manufactures."[2] As a result of the humiliating war which had just concluded, British statesmen had learned as never before the danger of dependence for naval supplies on the cordiality of northern powers. The nation had been brought to the brink of ruin, and this woeful situation was due in no small measure, as we have seen, to the ill condition of the bulwark fleet. It was not surprising, therefore, that the conclusion of hostilities inaugurated a new "stocktaking" of Empire. In Canada, as in the West Indies, the interests of sea-power were to be linked to those of trade.

Henceforth this study will be concerned with the develop-

his *Observations*, etc. See also p. 48. The ability of Britain to compete with France in this capacity helped to retain the vast bulk of the American trade; see Bemis, *Jay's Treaty*, pp. 28–30. Tucker Tracts, "Series of Answers," etc., etc., IV, Answer 5, p. 30.

[1] Sheffield, *Observations on the Commerce of America, 1784*.

[2] David Anderson, *Canada, a view of the importance of the British American Colonies*, Introduction.

ment of a new Canadian policy within the bounds of the Navigation System. That policy embraced three principal features. Firstly, the proposed scheme of substituting Canada for New England and the Middle States as a source of supply for the West Indies, following the failure of Sheffield and Pitt to secure a free trade ; secondly, the application to Canada of the old " colonial staple " policy under a system of bounties and preferential duties, as evidenced in the schemes for the growing of hemp and flax, and the regulations for cutting timber; thirdly, the alliance of diplomacy and commerce in the grand but visionary project of a vast American market zone, linked by the Canadian " vestibule " to England.

CHAPTER V

THE PROBLEM OF WEST INDIA SUPPLY

ALTHOUGH the Treaty of September 13, 1783, did not mark the beginning of the end for England's prosperity, as most wise men expected, it left an aftermath of troubles which did not find substantial solution until 1794. The main and immediate problem was the trade policy to be adopted towards the newly independent states, and again, the relations between these states and British overseas colonies on the same continent. Should the Navigation Laws be enforced as against a foreign country, or should the "palladium of English commerce" be expanded to include the new United States? Should the liberal principles of Adam Smith and of Shelburne be adopted, and the *status quo ante bellum* prevail; or should orthodox mercantilism, with Sheffield as its new high priest, place America beyond the pale of Navigation Laws, and seek adjustment in a new balance of Empire?

At the moment, the United States was a foreign country subject to the usual Navigation Laws, alien duties and restrictions. In the past she had played a vital part in supplying the West Indies and in absorbing much of their molasses, sugar and rum. But, as the law stood at present, the West India Islands were absolutely dependent on the remaining British continental colonies for provisions and cattle for sustenance, timber, boards and staves for industrial purposes, and varieties of naval stores for their shipping. On the other hand, Canada and the two adjoining colonies, Nova Scotia and Newfoundland had an almost exclusive legal preference on West India sugars, coffee, molasses and rum.

In the problem which thus confronted the British Government two questions were involved, one of theory and one of fact. Firstly, would a relaxation of the Navigation code which admitted the United States to trade mean any serious weakening of the established theory of monopoly as represented by the Navigation and Trade laws, and therefore be prejudicial to the prosperity of Great Britain ? Secondly, did actual conditions in Canada and Nova Scotia warrant the assumption that they could fully undertake West Indian supply, or did the situation require the assistance of the United States, theory or no theory ?

In 1762 the duel over Canada and Guadaloupe had found, ranged on one side, West India planters, who feared an accession of sugar colonies and the consequent drop in the price of sugar, London merchant groups with interests to push, and various theoretical believers in the north as a future source of naval supplies, furs, fish and even markets. On the other side, there were the monopolist trading and shipping classes, whose wealth depended on the West Indian sugar trade and whose ideal of national prosperity had a strangely individualist twist ; besides those who feared the expansionist policy involved in occupying a territory which might some day compete with the Mother Country. In this second duel of 1783–4 theoretical doubts of the wisdom of old mercantilism played an increasing part, as the students and disciples of Adam Smith slowly grew in numbers. But the issue was similarly governed by the action of " big interests," and influenced by sentiment both inimical and partial to the United States.

The planters, already fearful of the effects of a policy of restriction on their American trade, supported Pitt in his demands for free intercourse. The scanty supplies of Canada arriving either directly, or after a vessel had completed the triangular voyage—England to Canada, and thence to the West Indies—would cost immensely more than the products of the American trade. Furthermore, although with favourable seasons as in 1774 there might be a surplus of grain, a regular and sufficient supply could not be depended upon. Then, again, the navigation of the St. Lawrence was prohibited in winter by ice, and endangered in summer through strong currents, sunken reefs and fogs.[1]

[1] Governor Cadwallader Colden's description in 1724 remained literally true for 1784 : " The French labour under difficulties that no act or industry can remove. The mouth of the St. Lawrence and more especially the Bay of St. Lawrence lies so far north and is thereby so often subject to the tempestuous weather and thick fogs that the Navigation there is very dangerous and never

The planters were supported in these claims by those Whigs, who had sympathized with the American cause and who like Shelburne, were anxious to forget the past and lay the basis of a real peace; by the "œconomists" who pleaded the inutility of ancient Navigation Laws; and by new mercantile interests who favoured important relaxations of policy with regard to commerce.[1]

But a vehement opposition arose, which was to find a spokesman in John Baker Holroyd, first Earl of Sheffield. This famous agitator and propagandist based his stand on a complete denial of the dictum of Edmund Burke. Burke, when urging conciliation in 1775 had declared that the three branches of trade carried on by Great Britain with the continental colonies, West Indies and Africa, were so interwoven, that the attempt to separate them would tear to pieces the contexture of the whole, and if not entirely destroy would much depreciate the value of all the parts.[2] It became the task of Lord Sheffield and his ship-owner allies to demonstrate that Canada might occupy the place of the lost Middle and New England colonies as a source of West India supply, and thereby continue the old triangular trade within the bounds of the Old Colonial System.

attempted but during the summer months; the wideness of the Bay together with the many strong currents that run in it, the many shelves and sunken rocks . . . and the want of places for anchoring in the Bay, all increase the danger of this navigation, so that a voyage to Canada is justly esteemed much more dangerous than to any other part of America." *Documents relative to the Colonial History of New York*, Albany, 1856–87, Vol. V, pp. 630–1. Quoted by Brown, G.W., in "The St. Lawrence waterway in the 19th century," *Queen's Review*, Autumn, 1928.

[1] In opposition to Sheffield and the shipping groups, the mercantile interests were represented by Richard Champion, who contributed in support of their claims a pamphlet entitled *Considerations on the Present Situation of Great Britain and the United States*. See also "Observations of London Merchants on American Trade," a document contributed to the *American Historical Review* by Burnett, E. C., Vol. XVIII, pp. 769–80. For the planters Bryan Edwards wrote a pamphlet: *Thoughts on the late proceedings of Government respecting the Trade of the West India Islands with the United States of America.*

[2] Speech on Moving the Resolutions for Conciliation with the Colonies, March 22, 1775. *The Works of Edmund Burke* (World's Classics), Vol. II, p. 178. Note also a Petition and Memorial of the Council and Assembly of Jamaica, Dec. 4, 1784: "The Sugar Islands have been settled and have grown with their sister Colonies on the Continent of America; their interests are so united, the Reciprocity of Trade is such, that perhaps without it, neither would have arrived at their present consequence—most certainly the sugar colonies could not . . . the Productions of the former are so proper and well adapted for supporting and carrying on with any prospect of advantage the settlements of the latter, and so absolutely necessary in cases of emergency for the Preservation of the Inhabitants, that without such an Intercourse of Trade, the Sugar Colonies would sink into ruin." C.O. 137/85.

Sheffield had a considerable reputation as an authority on matters relating both to commerce and agriculture, and he had added to this prestige by his active aid in organizing militia for the suppression of the Gordon riots in 1780. His writings on commercial and political subjects were profuse and, with exceptions, good and scholarly work. Gibbon, who became his intimate friend in 1764, pays tribute to the reception of his *Observations on the Manufactures and Trade of Ireland* (1785). " The sense and spirit of his political writings," said the historian, " have decided the public opinion on the great questions of our commercial intercourse with Ireland."[1] Sheffield was strongly in favour of Union, and the book was intended to prove that Irish prosperity could only be maintained by a friendly connection with Great Britain.

But his most important work of propaganda was the *Observations on the Commerce of the American States*, which was published shortly after Pitt's attempt to introduce free trade legislation. It became the bible of the shipowners and mercantilist advocates of monopoly. According to the worshipping Gibbon—" The Navigation Act, the palladium of Britain, was defended and perhaps saved by his pen."[2] To Sheffield any relaxation of the mercantilist code would " affect our most essential interests in every branch of commerce . . . depriving the Navigation Laws of their efficacy and greatly reducing the naval power of Britain.[3] On the other hand, a monopoly of the West India trade would mean that the navy would be highly benefited, the business of ship-building greatly stimulated, and the number of seamen and artificers doubled."[4] " The American States," he declared, " are separated from us and independent, consequently foreign ; the declaring them such puts them in the only situation in which they can be. . . . Relying on those commercial principles and regulations under which our trade and navy have become so great, Great Britain will lose few of the advantages she possessed before the American States became independent, and with prudent management she will have as much of the trade

[1] *Memoirs ;* Edition 1837, p. 109.
[2] *Ibid.*, p. 108.
[3] *Observations*, etc., p. 3.
[4] *Ibid.*, Introduction, p. xxxviii.

as it will be her interest to wish for, without any expense to the State of Civil Establishment or protection."[1]

He preached the sufficiency of Canada, Nova Scotia and Newfoundland, and claimed that loyalty merited some reward, and that the migration to Canada of the American loyalists increased both their claims to consideration, and their ability to engage in West India trade.[2] The islands had subsisted throughout the war; how much happier would be their position now. Furthermore, should rebels be allowed to engross an important share of British shipping, when 60,000 seamen were out of work and a thousand transports rotting at anchor.[3] If American ships were allowed to take sugar from the British islands, they would in all likelihood convey much of it, not to America but to foreign countries. Thus Britain would be robbed of yet another branch of the carrying trade, and in all probability suffer serious competition with American ships for the freightage of goods to Great Britain.[4]

This, on the whole represented the attitude of all the shipowners and shipbuilders with their numerous merchant connections in London. They were actively reinforced by the Canada merchants and loyalists who wanted a monopoly of supplying the West Indies,[5] and by a public opinion which was definitely antagonistic to the development and progress of the United States.

Shelburne was still Prime Minister, and his attitude has already been explained in connection with the negotiation of the settlement of 1783. The failure of the treaty makers to include a reciprocal free trade agreement in the final articles was no fault of his own. As a true disciple of Adam Smith, he had, at the time, proclaimed the coming breakdown of monopoly

[1] *Ibid.*, etc., p. 78.

[2] Among the Chatham Papers is an interesting document, described as "Hints drawn up Anno 1780, when reconciliation with North America was expected." One of its recommendations is as follows: "Britain should appropriate the trade for grain and plantations' stores wanted in the sugar islands. These should be encouraged in raising part of their own provisions to guard against accidents. The introduction of American grain should be temporary and limited in circumstances of necessity or confined to barter. *The Canadians should be encouraged to erect flour mills*, and to send their flour immediately to the place of consumption without the medium of New York or Philadelphia." *Chatham MSS.*, 343.

[3] B.T., 5/1, fol. 120.

[4] Bryan Edwards, *op. cit.*, Bk. VI, Chap. IV, p. 498.

[5] Bemis, S. F., *Jay's Treaty*, p. 27.

and urged the benefits to be derived from a continued free intercourse with the United States. Largely on his advice, the preamble to the articles of the Provisional Agreement of November 30, 1782, had included the statement that, at a later date a treaty based on reciprocal freedom of commerce should be arranged " upon grounds of mutual advantage and convenience."

There is no doubt that Shelburne seriously intended to proceed with a commercial agreement of this sort, as soon as opportunity should allow.[1] Early in 1783 his friend, Thomas Pownall, had forcibly reminded him of this objective, and had also advised the continuance of the nurturing bounties previously conferred on colonial raw products.[2] The Prime Minister ignored the latter suggestion, but in a letter of reply, he asked him to review the statutes regarding commerce which might have to be revised in consequence of the Provisional Agreement of November 30. Pownall willingly undertook the case, and his final recommendations are worthy of summary.[3] To give legal definition to what he trusted would be America's new status, a test case should be referred to the Advocate-General stating the Provisional Agreement of November 30, 1782, the fundamental laws respecting Plantation trade, and the laws with regard to alien incapacities, prohibitions and restrictions. Three questions might form the basis of inquiry. Firstly, are the United States aliens ? Secondly, if so, can the King by a treaty of commerce stipulate an exemption from prohibitions and restrictions without the consent of Parliament? Thirdly, if not, how can Parliament best perform it ? Unfortunately Shelburne had not the parliamentary strength to follow Pownall's lead. His position in the House was being slowly undermined. His many enemies were plotting for his fall, and the ill-mated North-Fox partnership was able to bring this about on February 17, 1783.

The coalition ministry of Fox, North and Portland pursued a " hand-to-mouth policy," which is partly explained by the insecurity of its position and by the lack of any real construc-

[1] Wharton, *op. cit.*, Vol. VI, p. 203.
[2] Pownall to Shelburne, Jan. 30, 1783, Shelburne MS., Vol. 72, f, 86.
[3] Pownall to Shelburne, Feb. 2, 1783 ; Chatham MSS., 343, No. 274.

tive ability among its members.[1] In general they seem to have been influenced in their very half-hearted efforts by an antipathy to the late "plantations," and by a genuine belief in the established tradition of the sacredness of the Navigation Acts.

The man whom Lord North called in to assist him in framing regulations to govern the new colonial and American intercourse was William Knox. The North-Fox policy of vesting in the Crown, for a limited time, authority to regulate the commerce with America by means of orders-in-council may be said to have embodied the Under-Secretary's views on this subject. That policy was one of compromise,—of reconciling the immediate fact that Canada could not at the moment take the place of the American states as source of supply with the old-established theory of the integrity of the British Navigation System.

Knox, like Pownall, had a good grasp of colonial affairs. He had been associated with America since 1763, after an introduction to George Grenville had paved the way for his appointment as colonial agent in Great Britain for Georgia and East Florida. Georgia relieved him of his duties in 1765, as a result of his firm stand in defence of the Stamp Act. But he still took an interest in colonial administration, and appears to have been regularly consulted as to American policy. In 1770 he became Under-Secretary in the new Secretaryship of State for the Colonies. After the suppression of this department in 1782 he continued, as in this instance, to advise the Government on matters of moment.

Knox was one of a very few who did not lament the loss of the colonies.[2] It was no time for indecision and sorrowing, and a new balance of empire must be immediately sought and established. His long experience as a student of colonial affairs gave his opinions weight, and on this occasion they were fixed as steel. "Before I entered, I desired to know if the Administration agreed with me on the principle I meant

[1] Fox apparently favoured the opening of the West India trade to the Americans, but there were "many parties to please." Wharton, *op. cit.*, VI, p. 639; quoted Lingelbach, A. L., "The Inception of the British Board of Trade," *A.H.R.*, July, 1925, p. 204.

[2] "The loss of America may prove of negative, even positive benefit, to prevent emigration to America." *Extra-Official State Papers*, Part II, p. 53.

to found the regulations upon, which was, that it was better to have no colonies at all, than not to have them subservient to the maritime strength and commercial interests of Great Britain.[1] The navy was supported by commerce and commerce through the Navigation Laws." "I determined," he continues, "to oppose the whole American and West Indian interests, supported as they were by some of the members of the then Administration, and frame the regulations for the intercourse between the American States and the British West Indies, so as utterly to exclude the American shipping."[2] But the Under-Secretary was wise enough to realize as some of the more ardent members of the administration failed to realize—that Canada could not as yet possibly take the place of the Middle American colonies as *entrepôt*. Some relaxation of the Navigation code in favour of a direct American commerce was essential if the West Indies were to exist at all. So for the benefit of the Canada merchants and the shipping interests, Knox took pains to suggest that although some relaxations of the mercantilist order of things were necessary, they need be only temporary and experimental—"for it should be remembered that the object of this country is to exclude the communication of foreigners with our colonies, and that whenever our North American colonies shall be in a condition to supply wholly, the interference of foreigners is to be prevented."[3]

At the moment, lumber and provisions in quantity, naval supplies such as tar, pitch and turpentine, could not be obtained from Canada and Nova Scotia. They must, therefore, come from the United States. In the meantime every aid should be given to forward the Canadian production of wheat and flour, the raising of cattle and hogs and the development of the lumber industry. The erection of distilleries should be encouraged, as well as breweries for spruce beer, the famous antidote for scurvy.[4] In order that these colonies might sell their spirits as cheaply as the Boston distillers, the penny

[1] Knox, *op. cit.*, p. 54.

[2] *Ibid.*, p. 56 and appendices XIII and XVI; see also Knox MS., *Historical MSS. Commission Report*, 1909, p. 199. According to Knox, the regulations were carried through against the opposition of Fox and Burke, "and I thereby saved the navigation and maritime importance of this country." *Ibid.*

[3] Knox, *op. cit.*, Appendix XIII.

[4] See Chapter VII, p. 104.

excise tax on foreign molasses should be removed, "our own islands furnishing but an inconsiderable quantity."[1] With regard to this latter recommendation, Knox either underrated the strength or misinterpreted the feeling of the West Indian planters, who made it their objective during subsequent years to crush the infant distillery business in Canada.

The Ministry apparently accepted the judgments of the Under-Secretary, and on July 2, 1783, Parliament was prevailed upon to vest in the Crown, for a limited time, authority to regulate the commerce with America.[2] If Bryan Edward's statements be true, so extraordinary and extensive a grant to the executive power aroused little interest and excited little inquiry.[3] Even the West Indian merchants and resident planters appeared to have acquiesced on the ground that it was but a temporary measure. The Act was indeed only valid for six months; but it was renewed almost similarly until 1797.[4] Under its terms the importation into the West Indies of every species of naval stores, staves and lumber, live stock, flour and grain of all sorts, the growth of the American States, was confined to British shipping. To the United States, the West Indies were allowed to export rum, sugar, molasses, coffee, cocoa, nuts, ginger and pimento—also in British-built ships and paying the same duties and under the same regulations, as if exported to a British plantation colony. The importation of American meat, dairy produce and fish was forbidden altogether.

[1] Knox, *op. cit.*, Part II, pp. 45–6.

[2] "An Act for preventing certain instruments from being required from ships belonging to the U.S. of America, and to give to His Majesty for a limited time certain powers for the better carrying on of Trade and Commerce between the subjects of His Majesty's Dominions and the inhabitants of the said United States of America." *Minutes of the Board of Trade*, C.O. 5/2; *Privy Council Register*, *Geo. III*, XXI, fol. 316. See also *Parl. History*, XXIII, pp. 602–615, 640–646, 724–730, 762–767, 894–896.

[3] Bryan Edwards, *op. cit.*, Bk. V, Chap. IV, p. 496.

[4] This enabling Act was renewed by:—

23 Geo. III, c. 39.
24 Geo. III, cc. 2, 15.
25 Geo. III, c. 5.
26 Geo. III, c. 4.
27 Geo. III, c. 7.
28 Geo. III, c. 5 and 6.
29 Geo. III, c. 1.
30 Geo. III, c. 11.
31 Geo. III, c. 12.
32 Geo. III, c. 14.
33 Geo. III, c. 10.
34 Geo. III, c. 5.
35 Geo. III, c. 26.
36 Geo. III, c. 58.
37 Geo. III, c. 37.

See *Commons' Journals*, XXXIX, 362, 365, 368, 370, 377, 384, 386, 390, 392, 393, 394, 395, 409, 410, 411, 414, 415.

In final reckoning, the needs of the West Indies had been the deciding factor in the formulation of the Government's policy. Dogmatism in theory had bowed to the demands of the situation. As essential sources of supply, the United States were to be admitted to temporary membership within the Navigation System; but the monopoly of the carriage of their produce should still belong to Great Britain.

Unfortunately, a magnanimity, which permitted America to aid Canada in supplying the West Indies by means of British ships, was not likely to develop even a mild appreciation, and more than likely to involve reprisals. States such as New Hampshire, Massachusetts and Rhode Island attempted trade retaliation by actually prohibiting British vessels or those owned by British subjects to load any goods or merchandise the product of the growth of the United States, under penalty of seizure and condemnation. Others inflicted impositions in the nature of Port Duties, Tonnage Duties or Customs, arranged so as to give a preference to the shipping or manufactures of the American States or certain foreign nations, over those of Great Britain.[1]

On the whole such counter-attacks wrought havoc on the heads of those who endeavoured to enforce them. American prosperity depended on the West Indian market just as much as West Indian life depended on the neighbouring states' food supply. Early in 1784, the Board of Trade was able to satisfy the Ministry as to the safety of their policy. "If America excludes or prohibits our vessels from entering their ports," reported Inspector-General Irving, "they will deprive themselves of an annual market of at least £500,000 of their produce."[2]

Additional evidence confirmed official optimism.[3] In the French Islands only certain ports were open, and heavy duties were applied, particularly on fish, which amounted to about

[1] *Board of Trade Minutes*, C.O. 5/2, *passim*; David Anderson, *Origin of Commerce*, Vol. IV, p. 82. Maryland placed an imposition of 5*s.* a ton on British shipping, 2*s.* more than on any foreign, and 2 per cent ad valorem above the usual. Georgia prohibited all intercourse with the British West Indies, until the orders were revoked. South Carolina laid duties on West India produce from £50 to £100 higher than on that of foreign islands.

[2] *Board of Trade Minutes* (Evidence), April 1, 1784; B.T. 5/1, fol. 124.

[3] See "Comparative State of the Advantages America draws from her trade with the British Isles, beyond what she is allowed by Intercourse with the French Islands." (Undated); C.O. 5/8.

50 per cent. No bread or flour was admitted at all. Therefore a vent had to be found in the British colonies, or the supply would remain upon hand. The same applied to lumber. " She must send it to our market, and it is a certainty that our taking what supplies of those articles we want from her, will always insure to us an access to her ports, notwithstanding the ill-judged steps taken by some of the provinces to prevent it. Upon the whole, the advantages she will have in carrying on a trade with us even under our own regulations will ultimately end in her trading with us upon our own terms."[1] The Ministry could thus adopt a hostile attitude to American trade with little fear of danger to British commerce, and with apparently little risk to the West Indies.[2] If the Industrial Revolution had rendered England's welfare a matter of markets, to an even greater degree did the life of the new republic depend on foreign imports and the revenue derived from such.[3] The two countries were for the time being as inter-dependent as members of a friendly zollverein.

[1] *Board of Trade Minutes* (Evidence of William Knox, March 18, 1784), B.T. 5/1, fol. 35.

[2] Sufferings from famine in the West Indies during the subsequent period were by no means entirely due to the shipping monopoly but in a large measure to storm and hurricane; see C.O. 137/85, *passim*, and Governor Dalling to Germaine, Jamaica (Oct. 20, 1780, No. 80); C.O. 137/79.

In the summer of 1784 the ports were opened to foreign vessels carrying lumber and provisions for four months, and again until January 31, 1785. From then on they remained practically closed.

On Feb. 6, 1785, Lord Sydney wrote to Alured Clarke, the Lieutenant-Governor: " His Majesty does not disapprove of your having upon the pressing application of the Legislature extended the time limited for the admission of Lumber and Cattle from the American States to the 31st of January last. Hoped you have not found it necessary to grant further extension, but if absolutely expedient, and you have a second time acceded to the wishes of the Council and Assembly, it is His Majesty's express command that the admission of the articles above mentioned should determine upon the 31st of March next, and upon no account be extended after that day." C.O. 137/85.

Alured Clarke replied on Sept. 10, 1785: " I am determined to resist every application for the admission of Foreign vessels with provisions and lumber, contrary to the Royal Proclamation, as I entertain hopes that the necessity for such a measure will not be extreme and I am aware that nothing but extreme necessity can justify it." C.O. 137/85.

[3] According to Bemis, 90 per cent of American imports came from Great Britain; and the American revenue came mainly from a tariff on imports. To break relations would ruin three-fourths of American commerce. *Jay's Treaty*, p. 33.

The exports from Canada to England in 1787 amounted to but 1/119th of the sum of the exports to England from the United States. Reports as to Liverpool shipping show that British ships of 21,870 tonnage plied between

In the meantime the opposition to Fox's India Bill gave the King the opportunity he desired.[1] The coalition was ignominiously dismissed and the son of Chatham accepted the task of forming a government and facing the powerful opposition. He had the support of the King ; but only by grace of rescuing him from the Whigs. As against Fox, he represented the lesser of two evils, and therein lay his claim to royal favour, which at the time was not enough. Only the improprieties of Fox and the opposition coalition permitted the Ministry to live at all.

Even on so unstable a basis, Pitt did not delay in attempting to carry forward the liberal principles of free trade, which Shelburne had failed to introduce in 1782. On March 3, 1784, he introduced with some little haste a bill which gave to the Americans not only the privilege of unrestricted trade in their raw materials and manufactures with the West Indies, but also the right to share in the carrying trade between the Mother Country and the Islands.[2] It was this bold action on the part of Pitt which finally brought to a head the issue between Free Trade and Monopoly.

Sheffield's time had come; and his organizing tactics speedily aroused a fire-breathing opposition. Shipowners and their allies, societies of merchants and chambers of commerce stood up in their explosive wrath. In the Commons, William

that port and the United States in 1785, but only a tonnage of 2948 between it and British North America. Hertz, *Old Colonial System*, p. 188. See Allen's *Considerations on the present state of Intercourse between the Sugar Colonies and the U.S.A.* (1784), pp. 26 and 30.

[1] The Bill was carried by a large majority in the Lower House, but the King by means of intimidation was able to have it thrown out in the Lords by 19 votes. On Dec. 17th Pitt accepted the invitation to form a Ministry, and face the opposition. This interregnum lasted until March 25, 1784, when he dissolved, appealed to the country, and came back firmly established after an election which cost the Opposition 160 seats.

[2] Bill for the provisional Establishment and Regulation of Trade and Intercourse between the subjects of Great Britain and those of the United States of America : " Be it therefore enacted . . . that all statutes heretofore made to regulate the trade and commerce between Great Britain and British plantations in America ; or to prohibit the intercourse between the same, shall, so far as they regulate or prohibit the intercourse and commerce between Great Britain and the territories, now composing the said U.S. of America, wholly and absolutely cease." Quoted in Bryan Edwards, *op. cit.*, Bk. VI, Ch. IV, p. 491 ; Sheffield, *op. cit.*, p. 375 ; Chatham MS., 343.

For the course of Pitt's Bill in the Commons see *Commons' Journals*, XXXIX, 265, 270, 278, 284, 289, 243, 245, 301, 303, 308, 316, 320, 325, 346, 353, 362, 409, 429 ; *Parliamentary History*, XXIII, 602–15, 640–46, 724–30.

Eden declared the bill to be " of the greatest importance of any that he had seen in Parliament."[1] It would introduce a total revolution in our commercial system, which he was afraid " would be shaken to its very basis, and thus endanger the whole pile." The measure signified the repeal of the Navigation Act and therefore Great Britain might bid adieu to any Navigation Laws to bind Ireland. It would spoil the Irish provision trade, transfer a great part of the sugar-refining industry to America, and most dreadful of all, destroy the carrying trade. Six hundred British ships would become useless—" not only to the decrease of our revenue, but the absolute destruction of that great nursery for seamen." With forebodings of gloom strangely prophetic of nineteenth-century " Little Englandism " he contended that " if Quebec were not a flour country her prospect was melancholy indeed, for the unhappy and disgraceful destruction which had been made in all her hopes in the fur trade by the provisional articles had left her without any other resource."[2]

Both Edmund Burke and Charles Fox were mistrustful, and yet not anxious to condemn the measure out-right, until it had been further discussed in Committee.[3] Burke after a crushing rejoinder to Eden's cries of " ruin," found himself agreed with Pitt to the extent that he would treat the Americans not as aliens, but as fellow-subjects, as far as that were possible. On the other hand, he would establish his regulations rather by " an improvement of the old commercial system than by an introduction of a new one."

But die-hard advocates of monopoly with financial interests at stake provided resistance which proved too powerful. After the bill had been several times amended, Pitt was forced to withdraw it. Like Shelburne, the young Prime Minister was half a century ahead of his time. Pitt would have been wiser had he delayed in tackling so precipitately a problem on

[1] *London Chronicle*, March 7, 1784.

[2] See Debate of Feb. 2, 1785 ; *Parl. History*, XXV, p. 271.

The question at issue was that of relieving Newfoundland scarcity by admitting American provisions in British bottoms. Heretofore, a prohibitory measure had in effect confined the imports of food supplies to Canada. As a result bread had jumped from 20*s*. to 27*s*., to even 40*s*., a cwt., and there was imminent danger of famine. *Acts of Privy Council, Colonial*, Vol. V, pp. 410–14.

[3] Debate of March 7, 1784, *London Chronicle*, Vol. 53.

which there was so grave a diversity of opinion. In an age dominated by mercantilist interests and doctrinaire theory he attempted a revolution. Better had he followed the method of gradual reconstruction, which Huskisson was to adopt and carry to successful conclusion some forty years later.

When Pitt returned to power, he had definitely abandoned any idea of forcing his free trade views against the torrent of public opinion. Instead, therefore, of reviving the former provisional bill, one of his first tasks was to place before the newly constituted Committee of Trade and Plantations the whole problem of Navigation Laws and the question of Canada's ability to replace the Middle States as sources of supply.[1] In the meantime, since some immediate regulation was imperative, the Order-in-Council of the Fox-North coalition was prolonged for a year.[2]

The researches of the new Board of Trade were far-reaching and detailed ; and their first Minute Book is entirely occupied with a discussion of the subject.[3] The enquiry was presumably based on considerations of actual conditions, although it was obvious that the Committee were mainly guided by those whose evidence fitted in with accepted mercantilist theory. Against the testimony of Knox and Sheffield, proofs were presented of the total incapacity of Canada to give supply, particularly in wheat and flour, because of the constant uncertainty of the crops. On the other hand, it was claimed that the inhabitants were by no means equal to the task of consuming the rum necessary to promote the full cultivation of the Islands. In opposition to this viewpoint, Sir Guy Carleton, the former

[1] William III's Board of Trade finally disappeared after Burke's repeated assaults in July of 1782. The new Committee of Council on Trade and Plantations was formed on March 8, 1784, during the interregnum of Pitt, Dec. 17, 1783–March 25, 1784.

The " Mode of proceeding of the Committee of Council " was as follows : (1) The possibility of supplying the West India Islands from Canada, Nova Scotia and St. John's. Can they supply—or in what period can they ? (2) The mode of conveying supplies from the above provinces—whether by ships going from Great Britain, or by ships built in Nova Scotia or St. John's or by ships provided at the Islands or by Bermuda sloops ? (3) Whether the supply from the U.S. may not be brought to the Islands by some of the Modes of Conveyance above mentioned, at such price as may enable the West India planters to cultivate with sufficient profit, though not with so great advantage, as if the ships belonging to the subjects of the U.S. were allowed to be employed therein ? *Council of Trade Report*, March 13, 1784, B.T. 5/1, fol. 21.

[2] *Minutes of Board of Trade*, Dec. 26, 1783, C.O. 5/2.

[3] *Board of Trade*, B.T. 5/1.

Governor of Canada, was called as a witness. His prestige was still very high. It was Carleton who had placed the stamp of his influence and bias on the Quebec Act of 1774; and again in 1784, he became the counsellor and oracle, displaying an immoderation which must have been acceptable only because it was pleasing.

To him the possibility of sharing the West Indian carrying trade with the Americans appeared open to grievous objections.[1] " The opening of the trade for lumber and provisions with the United States in American bottoms would exceedingly injure the North American colonies remaining to Britain. If the Loyalists got possession of their lands, so as to begin cultivation immediately, Nova Scotia and Canada might be able to furnish the whole supply of lumber and provisions before the end of the year."[2]

" Large exports of wheat had been made prior to the war, from 200,000 to 400,000 bushels a year. There was no reason why future years should not witness similar averages according to the seasons. As to the lumber trade, plentiful supplies should be forthcoming, especially if Vermont and other parts of the ceded country about Lake Champlain could be included in the Canadian preference."[3] He admitted that the country laboured under a great disadvantage by reason of the distance from the sea and a difficult navigation route in the St. Lawrence. A vessel setting out in the spring was only able to make two trips, and was unable to return after the second. But there were grounds for optimism. If trade were confined to British bottoms, shipwrights, farmers and all concerned in West India trade would settle in Canada and Nova Scotia. But, on the contrary, if trade were laid open to the ships of the United States, it would have a contrary effect, and essentially check the growth and improvement of the province.[4]

[1] *Ibid.*

[2] Following the Peace, there was a rush of Tory Loyalists to British American territory. The numbers in Canada soon reached 25,000, and those in Nova Scotia and other British territory swelled the number to 60,000. See Van Tyne, C. H., *The Loyalists in the American Revolution*, Chap. XIII and Flick, *Loyalism in New York*, Chap. VIII, for a full detailed account of the migration to Canada.

[3] See Chapter VI.

[4] Carleton was a conscientious believer in the old colonial system. Strong pro-Canadian sentiment lent colour and emphasis to his orthodoxy, as the conclusion of the report makes apparent. " It is not in the Revolted provinces

Carleton presented his conclusions in the form of two alternatives, and mercantilist believers could choose but one way. "The struggle now to be decided involves a very important question, whether the United States or the remaining British colonies in America shall engross the benefits arising from a trade between the continent and the islands; if the former succeed, their cause and their interest, political as well as commercial, must increase; and in like manner, if the Loyalists prevail, they will contribute proportionately to their own and to the National Strength and prosperity; the only firm hold that Great Britain has upon the remains of the American Dominions is certainly by means of the Loyalists."[1]

In general, the Board of Trade accepted the Carleton point of view, and as against the anarchic tendencies of Pitt, they vindicated the policy of the Coalition. The argument which counted above all else, was that in favour of the shipping monopoly. The carrying trade must remain in British hands because it bred seamanship and naval power. By excluding American ships from the ports of the West Indies, it was estimated that Britain would find full employment for as many additional vessels as America formerly employed in that commerce, and would reap all the profits which America reaped, of which the freightage alone came to £245,000 annually.[2] The privilege of supplying the islands belonged by ancient right to Great Britain and her loyal colonies. Evidence pointed hopefully to the fact that the loyal colonies would soon be able to supply a large proportion of the lumber and provisions which the West Indies required, and in all probability would in three years supply the whole.

Pitt abided by that decision, which was absolutely in accord with the Order-in-Council of 1783. The Enabling Acts should

alone that a Republican spirit is to be found, but the taint has in some degree spread to other parts of America, and even to the West Indies, which has probably contributed to influence some of the planters on the present occasion —who under pretence of getting supplies from the continent at a cheaper rate, and finding a readier market for their produce, have secured the general concurrence of such as have no direct views of a political nature, and who look no further than to objects of immediate profit, not aware that the consequences of their success in the present application must eventually be not beneficial, but on the contrary dangerous to themselves by diminishing the national Resources of Naval Strength, on which the safety of the British Islands so essentially depends."

[1] *Board of Trade Minutes*, Whitehall, March 16, 1784; B.T. 5/1.

[2] Bryan Edwards, *op. cit.*, Bk. VI, Chap. IV, p. 509.

remain a temporary expedient—a concession to the immediate needs of the West Indies—which might be revoked whenever Canada should find herself capable of undertaking full supply.

It is apparent that the Government had based much of their hopes for a Canadian *entrepôt* on the incoming Loyalist settlers. But could they, as Sheffield and Carleton seemed to presuppose, overturn the lethargic methods of a century and convert a country of wilderness and trading posts into a bursting land of harvest fields and flour mills ? Would future history justify the claims of the Board of Trade, and redeem the principle of the integrity of the British Navigation System ? The answer to this question forms a significant commentary on the Sheffield triumph in 1784.

During the first year of the Peace, there had been a fair export of flour to Halifax, Newfoundland and even to the British Isles ;[1] and the repeal of the ordinance of 1780 prohibiting export was considered.[2] For the time being, however, the inrush of Loyalists tested rather than contributed to the food resources of the province.[3] The risks of climate were still too formidable to be chanced, and the Governor adopted the temporary expedient of licensing for export. Council Minutes relate that many licences were petitioned for, and granted—particularly for Newfoundland and Nova Scotia export,—and that considerable quantities of foodstuffs found their way across the border.[4]

By 1785 conditions had become more or less settled following the usual confusion and stagnation of a post-war period. The crops of 1784 had been bountiful, and the harvest of the year

[1] C.O. 42/12, fol. 240. For extracts of *Imports and Exports* into the Province of Quebec for the years, 1783–4–5 see C.O. 42/11, fol. 82.

[2] *Council Minutes*, June 17, 1783 ; C.O. 45/4. According to government census, the population in 1783 was 113,012 ; land under cultivation, 1,569,818 acres ; and seed sown, 383,349 bushels.

[3] Haldimand to Sydney, London, March 3, 1785, enclosing a table of rations estimated as necessary for the incoming Loyalists. C.O. 42/47, fol. 91.

[4] All the petitions for licences to export provisions to Newfoundland, Nova Scotia and West Indies, seem to have been granted without exception. On June 17 it was ordered that an advertisement be inserted in the next *Quebec Gazette* by the Secretary of the Province, notifying that licences to export provisions would be granted to individuals applying to the Governor and Council. (Minutes of Council upon State Business from June 17, 1783, to the 1st day of May, 1784) ; C.O. 45/4. The food products consisted chiefly of biscuit, oats, oatmeal, flour, peas, wheat, sheep, pigs and bullocks.

augured well. The time seemed ripe for an attempt to set definitely in motion a West Indian trade.[1]

Under the limited licensing plan, some provisions were shipped; but the total amount to the West Indies was insignificant. Only four or five vessels a year exchanged, and in 1788, only one or two.[2] Moreover, a considerable part of the cargoes consisted of staves, heading and hoops for rum casks, and lumber and shingles for construction work.[3] Even a recent reciprocity agreement with the West Indies[4] failed to stimulate any notable increase in the products of the soil, or benefit an exchange. Nova Scotia was still forced to import provisions, staves, boards and shingles from the United States, "a clear proof," said David MacPherson, who might have correctly included Canada, that "after a trial of seven years, Nova Scotia is very far indeed from being able to supply the West Indies with provisions; and, what is more surprising in an uncultivated country covered with trees, that it even stands in need of lumber for building houses and making casks for the fish, which are likely to continue the principal article of trade."[5]

A further blow to hopes of a West Indian Trade came in 1789. The crops of the previous year had failed utterly and distress was widespread. Around Montreal, people were eating horses, or even animals that had died of want.[6] Despite the flood of petitions urging direct importation, and Carleton's[7] own urgent plea for freedom to open ports to American products in British bottoms,[8] the Board of Trade coldly observed

[1] *Minutes of Council*; C.O. 45/11, fol. 163.

[2] *Council Minutes* (Evidence submitted to a Committee of Council); C.O. 45/11, fol. 163–7. See evidence of Adam Lymburner, purporting to be based on Custom House Books: There was a good export of wheat, 221,931 bus. in 1777, which fell off slightly in 1788; C.O. 42/88, fol. 127. See also C.O. 42/66 for table of exports.

[3] Sydney to Clarke, Whitehall, April 9, 1785. C.O. 137/85; which gives an account of the number of vessels and their cargoes from Canada and Nova Scotia entered at Jamaica between July 2, 1783, and Feb. 2, 1785. See also Bryan Edwards, *op. cit.*, Bk. VI, Chap. IV, p. 519 (footnote).

[4] See Chap. VI, pp. 91–2.

[5] MacPherson, D., *op. cit.*, Vol. IV, p. 212.

[6] MacPherson, D., *op. cit.*, Vol. IV, p. 188. See also Memorial of Alexander Henry, May 30, 1789; C.O. 45/9; Quebec Council Minutes, June 2, 1789; C.O. 45/10; and Quebec Council Minutes, July 14, 1789; C.O. 45/11; Memorial of Merchants of London, July 14, 1789; C.O. 42/66; also Council Minutes, April 2, 1789, with regard to a bill for public relief, C.O. 45/7.

[7] Carleton became Lord Dorchester on Aug. 21, 1786.

[8] Dorchester to Hawkesbury, Feb. 14, 1789; B.T. 5/5, fol. 279; see also two letters of Lord Hawkesbury read before Board of Trade, June 12, 1789,

that, " upon the supposition of the Illegality of any importation by sea or coastwise of the produce of the American States, nothing could apologize for the smallest contravention of the Letter and intent of the Statute, prohibiting that commerce with those States, but the most incontestable proof of the danger of the lives of His Majesty's subjects by a general dearth, and that even then, the importation ought to be with all such restrictions as would limit the Introduction of the Supplies in their Nature and Quantities to the relief, which the real necessities of the colony required."[1]

Such incontestable proofs were not wanting. Finally, although tardily, the Board of Trade, which seems to have wielded a direct influence on this matter, reported in favour of the need for " sea importation of provisions, to be confined to flour, meal, biscuit, rice and Indian corn."[2] In July, the King was empowered to permit by an Order-in-Council the importation of bread, flour, Indian corn and livestock into Canada from the United States in times of scarcity,[3] notwithstanding an inconvenient statutory prohibition of 1788.[4] Not until the next year was a formal bill drafted, giving the Governor a free hand in an emergency to import for a limited time only, provisions in British ships by sea or the St.Lawrence.[5]

If British statesmen had based their hopes for a future all-British triangular trade monopoly on the capacity of Canada to fill one corner, it would appear from the past brief survey that they were to be disappointed. In any event, even had

re the opening of Port St. Johns for the free importation of provisions by Lake Champlain and the River Sorel—" and submitting the expediency of lodging a power with the Government of Canada to allow the Importation of Wheat and Flour from the American States into the Province of Quebec by Sea." *Board of Trade Minutes*, B.T. 5/5.

Dorchester on his own initiative opened up the seaports to American provisions in British bottoms. Letter of June 6, 1789; C.O. 42/12, p. 393. Dorchester to Hawkesbury, Que., Sept. 30, 1789, on reasons for opening free ports; B.T. 5/6. By Geo. III, c. 58, it was decreed that " In consideration of the scarcity in the province of Quebec, 2000 quarters of wheat, 2000 sacks of flour, and 8000 quarters of peas were permitted to be carried to that province, whatever price they might be at "—which thus represented a modification of the Corn Laws, 13 Geo. III, c. 43.

[1] Report received by the Quebec Council, June 2, 1789; C.O. 45/10.

[2] Report of July 14, 1789; C.O. 45/10.

[3] 29 Geo. III, c. 16.

[4] 28 Geo. III, c. 6.

[5] 30 Geo. III, c. 1, drafted Jan. 14, 1790; *Board of Trade Minutes*, B.T. 5/6. Passed April 1, 1790; see MacPherson, Vol. IV, p. 202.

the country blossomed to their ambitions, it is strange to suppose that she could have built up a trade in competition with the less distant Middle States. Despite all the casuistry of Westminster, the United States held the advantage. Their proximity to the islands and the natural benefit of an uninterrupted navigation, were insurmountable barriers in the way of the Canadian navigator, as well as the lumber and flour manufacturer.[1] Under the Enabling Acts, the West Indies, fortunately for their existence, could obtain naval stores and provisions under the same conditions as if they had been imported from a British colony in British bottoms. Beyond the fact that Britain monopolized the shipping, there was practically the usual pre-war freedom of trade with the exception of the enumerated commodities, meat, dairy produce and fish.

An additional handicap lay in the fact that the American trade through time had become highly organized and systematically regulated. Canada knew nothing of the proper assortment of cargoes, and little about the preparation of lumber. She managed to export wheat intermittently, but flour was even less a steady article of trade, for there were only three or four mills in the whole province.[2] Furthermore, distance rendered her inadept at gauging the West Indies market. Large stocks on hand in the islands produced low prices, while an exhaustion of stores might send prices sky-high. The Canadian shipper could only speculate on the market, and set sail in hope.[3]

It is apparent, therefore, that, as a source of West Indian

[1] See Report of Committee of Council on Commerce and Police, Que., Jan. 29, 1787; C.O. 42/50. There was also the fact of smuggling in American ships. Nelson, while stationed as a junior officer at St. Christopher, makes a reference to this circumvention of the Navigation Laws. " The longer I am upon this station, the worse I like it. Our Commander has not that opinion of his own sense, that he ought to have. He is led by the advice of the islanders to admit the Yankees to a trade; at least to wink at it. . . . I for one, am determined not to suffer the Yankees to come where my ship is; for I am sure, *if once the Americans are admitted to any kind of intercourse with these Islands, the views of the Loyalists in settling Nova Scotia are entirely done away. They will first become our carriers, and next have possession of our islands, are we ever again embroiled in a French war.*" As related by Horatio Nelson to Wm. Lockyer, Jan. 15, 1785. *Dispatches and Letters of Lord Nelson* (edited by Sir. H. Nicolas), Vol. I.

[2] There were three mills at Quebec, and one at Montreal, principally used for flour for the West Indies and Newfoundland. B.T. 5/1, fols. 46–7.

[3] See Adam Anderson, *op. cit.*, Vol. IV, p. 90.

supply, the province had failed lamentably.[1] It had not even qualified to maintain itself. A series of bad seasons had been the greatest handicap; but the inertia of the "habitants," and the inevitable slowness with which the Loyalists adjusted themselves to new surroundings proved additional obstacles in the way of rapid agricultural progress. Exigencies of climate and pioneer settlement were still too powerful to be overcome with aught but patience. Both Carleton and Sheffield had ambitiously under-estimated the difficulties and over-estimated the ability of the Loyalist immigrants to work miracles. With the growing recognition of this error, there vanished, in the words of Bryan Edwards, "golden dreams and delusive promises."[2]

[1] According to Bryan Edwards there were shipped in the year 1790 from the United States to Nova Scotia alone, 540,000 staves and heading, 924,980 ft. of boards, 285,000 shingles and 16,000 hoops; 40,000 barrels of bread and meal and 80,000 bushels of grain—"an irrefragable proof that Canada had no surplus of either lumber or grain beyond her own consumption, or undoubtably the Canadian market would have been resorted to, in preference to that of the United States"; Bryan Edwards, *op. cit.*, Bk. VI, Chap. IV, p. 518.

[2] *Ibid.*

CHAPTER VI

RUM AND THE TRIANGULAR TRADE

In spite of conflicting evidence the Board of Trade had recommended and the Government had decided that Canada was fitted to take her place as a contributor to West India support and a base in the triangular trade. It was not altogether a new departure, for the principle of West India-Canada exchange had been established in 1774. Passed that year in conjunction with the Quebec Act, the Quebec Revenue Act fulfilled a double purpose. Influenced by the exigencies of a period which had helped to mould the former, it became the first important modification of the old mercantile system as applied to Canada. In this sense it can be viewed purely as a fiscal measure—an Act "to establish a fund towards defraying the charges of the administration of Justice and Support of the Civil Government within the Province of Quebec."[1] From a second point of view it may be called a trade regulation, the object of which was to direct British Canadian trade into definite and regulated channels.

The Act repealed the old Crown duties on the importation of wine, rum and brandy along with the *ad valorem* duty on dry goods and established new discriminating duties on molasses and spirituous liquors in their place.[2] The peculiar importance of the new tariff lay, however, in the fact that the revenue

[1] 14 Geo. III, Chap. 88.

[2] The rates were as follows :—

For every Gallon of Brandy, or other Spirits, of the *Manufacture* of Great Britain, Three-pence.

For every Gallon of Rum, or other Spirits, which shall be imported or brought from any of His Majesty's Sugar Colonies in the *West Indies*, Sixpence.

For every Gallon of Rum, or other Spirits, which shall be imported or brought from any other of His Majesty's Colonies or Dominions in *America*, Nine-pence.

For every Gallon of Foreign Brandy or other Spirits of Foreign Manufacture, imported or brought from Great Britain, One Shilling.

For every Gallon of Rum or Spirits, of the Produce or Manufacture of any of the Colonies or Plantations in America, not in the Possession or under the Dominion of His Majesty, imported from any other Place, except Great Britain, One Shilling.

For every Gallon of Molasses and Syrups, which shall be imported or

derived should be applied to the support of the internal administration of the province by the governing body concerned.[1] There must be no more cries of "taxation without representation," no recurrence in Canada of the Boston Tea Party, that prologue to a tragedy which had yet to come.

The significance of the Act as a trade regulation depended in the first place on the importance of the fur trade, and that in turn depended on the regular flow of the West India product—rum Rum was regarded as a prime necessity to northern peoples, and to the French Canadian habitant it was an essential food product. To the British trader it was an absolutely indispensable article of commerce.[2] Following the American Revolution, its importance increased correspondingly with competition to the southward, as British Canadian traders endeavoured to retain the trade of the Old North West with cheap manufactures and gallons of rum.[3] The Indian trappers

brought into the said Province, in Ships or Vessels belonging to His Majesty's Subjects in Great Britain or Ireland, or to His Majesty's Subjects in the said Province, Three-pence (plus 1*d.* Old Duty).

For every Gallon of Molasses and Syrups, which shall be imported or brought into the said Province, in any other Ships or Vessels, in which the same may be legally imported, Sixpence; and after those Rates for any greater or less Quantity of such Goods respectively. Shortt and Doughty, *op. cit.*, I, p. 577.

[1] It may be noted that the Act in no way cancelled the Crown Territorial and Casual Revenues, Fines, Rents and other royal dues, which prior to the conquest had belonged to the French king. Some years later these royal revenues became the subject of a warm discussion in the Canadian Council. If the Quebec Revenue Act had never been passed, could they have been legally collected? The disputants were promptly quashed, but the royal rights to Casual and Territorial Revenues remained a source of dispute and irritation well into the nineteenth century. See *Minutes of Council* for 1787; C.O. 45/8.

[2] In October, 1790, a petition signed by all the important merchant companies asked for an amendment of the ordinance of 1777, which restricted the sale of spirituous liquors to the Indians. "If the first is restrained it will transfer the trade to the Americans and Spaniards, because it is well known that the savages will have liquor somewhere, and if they cannot get them from us will go where such restrictions are unknown." *Council Minutes*, Dec. 2, 1790; C.O. 45/12. In his recent book *The American-Indian Frontier*, (N.Y., 1928), Mr. W. C. McLeod draws attention to the deliberate use of rum by European powers at an earlier period to sap the energies of tribes allied to their rivals.

[3] The demands of thirst are indicated by the table of expenditure of rum at Niagara from May 11, 1777, to May 10, 1778:—

	Gals.	*Pints.*
Garrison	757	–
Navy	2025	1
To Indians out of King's Store ...	3736	4
To Indians from Ed. Pollard ...	623	–
	7141	5

and hunters were the key to the situation. The safety of the province, according to Haldimand, depended entirely upon their exertions, " which ever have and ever will be governed by the Presents they Receive, the enormity of which originated in gaining their affections—so powerfully and at first so successfully opposed by the Rebels."[1] By the safety of the province, Haldimand also meant the security of the fur trade. It is no exaggeration to say that its successful pursuit depended entirely on cheap goods and liberal supplies of rum. Furs and peltries dominated the Canadian scene almost as powerfully as cotton a generation later was to rule the destinies of the southern United States.[2]

But if the demand for rum should be made to fulfil the needs of a revenue, it was also persuaded to play a part in furthering the success of the British Navigation System. The Quebec Revenue Act was aimed to link up Canada more definitely as a pivotal corner in the triangular trade. Freight and insurance charges were nearly the same from the West Indies to Quebec as from England to Quebec.[3] By making rum cheaper to import from England than from the West Indies, a system of trade could be promoted whereby the West Indies would send to England, rum, molasses, sugar and coffee—England to Canada, chiefly rum and English manufactures, and finally—Canada to the West Indies, provisions, lumber, staves and naval stores, articles on which the partisans of Lord Sheffield had based their faith and hopes. By placing a 6*d.* duty on rum and 4*d.* on foreign molasses imported directly from the islands, and by admitting rum to Britain duty free, the Government arranged that this vital product should through preference be purchased from England.

The advantages to be derived from this roundabout trade were reckoned in terms of shipping and sea power. Britain's naval strength was considered to rest on two commercial bases, fisheries and the carrying trade. These two industries provided the twin schools for English seamen. " Our fisheries,

[1] Quebec, Oct. 21, 1781 ; Treasury 64/115.

[2] " The Indian Trade is ever of first magnitude in the internal and external commerce of Canada," read the celebrated Report of the Merchants on Commerce and Police of Jan., 1787. " It must pay not only for British manufactures consumed by the Indians but serve as capital and profitable remittance on account of our consumption at large." C.O. 42/50, *passim.*

[3] *Ibid.*, fol. 330.

domestic and foreign," said Edward Long, "are the prize for contest, the object for national emulation and the grand point to which our policy and our exertions ought to be directed."[1] Concerning the carrying trade, the Navigation Laws enunciated the principle that the more long voyages made, the greater the number of ships and sailors employed, and in consequence the higher efficiency of the British Navy.[2] In an age of sailing ships when a sailor's skill was the result of long continuous experience at sea, and when naval stores were largely interchangeable between the Navy and the mercantile marine,[3] one was to a much greater degree than to-day, "a nursery" for the other. Thus, in the case of the West Indies trade it was assumed that the nation would be more benefited by the additional British shipping employed in a long and circuitous route by way of Britain, than by equalizing the duties and lowering the price of rum.

Furthermore, the influence of the merchant class may be noted in a more practical way. Past experience had taught generations of West India merchants the wise necessity of obliging the planter to send his rum to the British market in payment of his debts. Under these circumstances there was less temptation to divert it to speculation in America or in any other country.[4]

Until after the American Revolution, Canada had little opportunity to take the part for which the Revenue Act was presumed to have prepared her. As has been observed in a previous chapter, the country was handicapped by its geographical position, and during the period of the war had remained hopelessly dependent on home supply for provisions as well as for rum and other vital necessities. Its position was that of the feeble infant requiring parental nourishment and care, rather than that of a potentially responsible member of the triangular partnership.

[1] Ed. Long, *Observations on West Indies Trade*, 1784. (Brit. Mus.) Add. MS. 18274.

[2] In his Introduction to *Observations*, etc., *op. cit.*, Sheffield remarks that the business of ship-building will be greatly increased in the British dominions, the number of artificers will be doubled and sailors increased. "All this, however, absolutely depends on the support of our Navigation Laws. If these laws should be relaxed, the reverse will be our fate."

[3] Martin, Chester, *Empire and Commonwealth, Studies in Governance and Self-Government in Canada*, p. 3.

[4] C.O. 42/50, fol. 330, *passim*.

The really active continental partner had hitherto been New England and the middle colonies. Yet even their position within this particular branch of the old colonial system had been one of doubtful efficiency. Instead of representing a pivotal point in a three-cornered circuit, they may be regarded rather as a shuttle within the system. In other words, the triangular trade was in reality a trade of separate distinct parts, rather than a process of single continuous voyages on the principle of perpetual motion. There was direct trade from Great Britain to America, and direct trade from Great Britain to the Islands, with sometimes only one voyage per annum.[1] Occasionally a vessel returned *via* the West Indies with freight and ballast, but on the whole, roundabout voyages were rare. Subjected to long experiment, they had not paid.[2] It proved to be a speculative business to load a bulky cargo of lumber for the islands, and take back to England the compact return cargo of rum, which in comparison might not afford more than light ballast.[3]

As a result, the important West India–American carrying trade was practically monopolised by the New England states. In little single-decker sloops or schooners, ranging from 60 to 100 tons, they journeyed back and forth in well-marked lanes, making two and often three voyages a year.[4] More than three-fourths were American built,[5] although occasional vessels were owned by Englishmen at home. The exchange in provisions, lumber and staves, with sugar, rum, molasses and coffee in return was effected much more cheaply by these smaller and less expensively operated colonial craft.[6] Occasionally Ameri-

[1] Observations on West India Trade, Quebec, Jan. 3, 1790; C.O. 45/11, fol. 163.

[2] Evidence of Thomas Atkinson, Inspector of Customs, B.T. 5/1, fol. 13.

[3] " There was not sufficient vent in Europe for West India rum, the whole importation of that article into Great Britain and Ireland being little more than half the quantity consumed in America," Bryan Edwards, *op. cit.*, Bk. VI, Chap. IV, p. 489. An average yearly consumption of British West Indies rum by America before the war was 2,800,000 gals., and the quantity of molasses was 250,000 gals. *Ibid.*

[4] B.T. 5/1, fol. 13. According to Bryan Edwards the actual number of voyages in any one year was 533, occupying 3339 seamen, including negroes; *op. cit.*, Bk. VI, C. IV, p. 488.

[5] B.T. 5/1, fol. 13.

[6] *Ibid.* The single deckers were rarely employed in trans-Atlantic voyages because of high insurance rates. For details of trade, see Board of Trade, Minutes of Committee of Trade, Evidence of Inspector-General Irving, March 30, 1784; B.T. 5/1, fol. 120. Also see note, B.T. 5/1, fol. 12, and Bryan

can owners sent 200-ton ships to the islands and thence to England, but more frequently these were sent as remittances and sold to the correspondent on arrival.[1]

It is therefore obvious that the triangular trade in the sense of continuous circuitous voyages was seriously interrupted by an American colonial carrying trade. In largely eliminating the roundabout voyage for the larger ocean vessels the colonies were to a degree negativing the dogma of the triangular trade, —triple voyages, triple freights, more sailors and greater sea power.

The Treaty of 1783 swept away this colonial control of carriage, but the trade itself was continued almost without interruption by means of a series of Enabling Acts which gave the monopoly of carriage to British shipping. Nevertheless, Sheffield and his followers had declared Canada's ability to take the place of the old colonies as a truly subordinate pivotal point in a new triangular circuit. The Quebec Revenue Act had laid the basis for that development. Sooner or later Canada, according to her advocates, must redeem the principle of the triangular trade and maintain in the words of Burke " the contexture of the whole."

Yet almost at once the principle of the " carrying trade "— longer voyages, more ships, and more seamen—came into conflict with colonial ambitions for a direct trade. London merchants interested in furs and fish, Canadian exporters engaged in the lumber and milling industries, and West Indian planters whose fortunes in many instances depended on rum, were anxious to develop an efficient inter-colonial commerce in the manner of the late colonies. They objected to a scheme which made Jamaica and Quebec mere ports-of-call in a more expensive roundabout system of single voyages. The Quebec Revenue Act of 1774 became the object of their attack. It was in no way an attack against a principle of the Navigation System as represented by the triangular trade. Both sides were wise enough to realize that their case depended on a reconciliation of their private demands with the larger, national interests of shipping and sea power.

Edwards, *op. cit.*, Bk. VI, Chap. IV, p. 487, for an account of the total import from North America into the British West Indies for the years 1771, 1772 and 1773.

[1] B.T. 5/1, fol. 13.

The West Indian groups were quite favourable to a roundabout trade in rum so long as their Canadian trade was not obliterated by smuggling, or by foreign competition in the form of cheap molasses for home distillation. The Canadian merchants, too, appreciated the significance of the triangular trade in the national life, but maintained that in competition with American traders, the fishing and fur trade depended absolutely on quantities of cheap molasses and cheap rum. On the other hand, a direct Canada-West Indies exchange would give new incentive to native industry; it would protect the fur trade and induce a prosperity which would in turn stimulate a triangular trade in British manufactures, Canadian lumber and provisions, and finally, in West Indian sugar, coffee and rum. In short, both sides favoured the economical, direct exchange of natural produce within the triangular system—only the planters maintained that the Canadian distilleries should not compete with West Indian rum—and the Canadian exporters that the islands should provide a more assured market for Canada's infant industries.

Prior to 1775, the annual export of rum direct to Canada, Nova Scotia and Newfoundland probably averaged under 100,000 gallons, of which Canada's share had been less than half.[1] The Quebec Revenue Act had profoundly altered a growing trade. In the first place, as we have noticed, it laid a 6*d.* duty on rum imported directly from the islands, whereas rum imported by way of Great Britain was duty free. Secondly, it laid a duty of 4*d.* on all molasses carried in British or Irish shipping. Since there was thus no tariff discrimination between British or foreign molasses, a decided preference of taste for the foreign product meant that the Canadian supply was almost entirely obtained from the French and Dutch colonies.[2]

Canadian-made rum lessened both the direct and the triangular commerce because it was cheaper. The distillation of

[1] See *Report of Privy Council* of May 31, 1784 (p. 28); C.O. 137/87. The total amount imported directly before the war was 998,000 gallons, but from 1775 to 1786 only 859,500. C.O. 42/12, fol. 215.

[2] *Ibid.* See also a Memorial of West India Merchants to Lord Commissioners of Treasury regarding the introduction of Rum and Molasses into Canada, March 9, 1786 (included with Extract of Resolutions of Standing Committee of West Indian Planters and Merchants, London Tavern, April 5, 1787); C.O. 42/12, fol. 9.

molasses cost from 6*d.* to 7*d.* a gallon. This, added to the import price and the 4*d.* duty, brought the gallon of Quebec distilled rum to about 2*s.* 2*d.*[1] On the other hand, the best Jamaica brand imported directly cost 3*s.* and cheaper varieties 2*s.* 9*d.* Jamaica rum imported by way of the triangular route through Great Britain cost the same as if imported directly, but the cheaper varieties could be purchased in this manner for 2*s.* 5*d.*[2] It is apparent, therefore, that the roundabout triangular trade in West Indian rum through England was made to work on a preference of about 4*d.* over direct importation. But this trade was largely interrupted by the fact that the home-distilled product was 3*d.* cheaper than West Indian rum imported by way of the triangular route.

According to Jamaica petitions, this disparity was slowly undermining their rum trade. In 1787 there were four distilleries in Quebec with a capacity of 420,000 gallons. Heretofore, their production had been only half that amount,[3] but even that quantity almost equalled the supply of spirits imported from Great Britain, and was two-thirds greater than the quantity imported directly.[4] Carefully prepared evidence

[1] The Jamaica planters estimated the price of British West Indian rum imported directly at 2*s.* 10*d.*; that distilled in Canada at 2*s.*; C.O. 137/87.

[2] Rum distilled in the province was—

6*d.* less than that imported directly from the Leeward and Windward Isles.

9*d.* less than that imported directly from Jamaica.

2*d.* or 3*d.* less than that imported directly from the Leeward and Windward Isles through Britain.

9*d.* less than that imported from Jamaica through Britain; C.O. 42/12, fols. 193–4.

[3] C.O. 42/51, fol. 471; also Dorchester to Sydney, Nov. 10, 1787, C.O. 42/12, fol. 171, also Report of Committee appointed to enquire into the present state of the Intercourse between the British West India Islands and His Majesty's Colonies in North America, respecting the Import of Rum and Molasses into these Colonies, Jan. 8, 1788; C.O. 137/87.

[4] The import from British West India Islands into Quebec in 1786 (duty 6*d.*):

	1404 puncheons or	138,637 gallons.
Import from Great Britain for same period (duty free)	2164 puncheons or	207,744 gallons.
Total ...	3568 puncheons or	346,381 gallons.

Import of molasses from French West Indian Isles and Dutch Settlements (duty 4*d.*):

Guadaloupe and Martinique	232 puncheons.
Hispaniola	1628 ,,
Surinam	252 ,,
	2112 puncheons (or about 211,000 gallons).

showed that the importation of foreign molasses was slowly increasing and that the importation of West Indian rum was diminishing in the same proportion—" and in all probability in a year or two, there will be little or no rum imported into Canada."[1]

The suggested remedy for this lamentable state of affairs, as submitted by the planters' committee, was simple. Firstly, the duty on British West India rum imported into Canada should be either taken off or greatly reduced. Secondly, the Canadian distilleries should be suppressed and the erection of others prohibited. Thirdly, the duty on foreign molasses imported into the North American colonies should be increased.[2]

The Quebec merchants had been giving consideration to the same problem, at the request of their Legislative Council.[3] They agreed with the planters, that the *6d.* duty on imports from the islands acted as a prohibition to direct intercourse, as well as handicapping the triangular trade. It placed a premium on the introduction of a foreign commodity, molasses, which inevitably had a tendency to drain the province of its specie without saving anything to the consumer.[4] The effect was not only to injure the revenue, but greatly to check the exports of flour and other produce of the soil. On the other hand, the colony must have cheap rum. Basing their recommendations, therefore, largely on the merchants' evidence, the Legislative Council recommended that, if it was found necessary to make any alteration of the law in favour of the West

According to the report " each gallon of molasses distilled at Quebec or Montreal produces an equal quantity of spirit of the standard of Windward Island Rum, to which standard they reduce rum from this island." C.O. 137/87.

[1] *Ibid.*

[2] Memorial of West India merchants to Lords Commissioners of the Treasury regarding the introduction of Rum and Molasses into Canada, March 9, 1786 (included with Extract of Resolutions of the Standing Committee of West India planters and merchants, London Tavern, April 5, 1787) ; C.O. 42/12, fol. 9 ; B.T. 5/5 (Copy Reference), Whitehall, March 31, 1788 ; and C.O. 45/6 (Copy referred to the Quebec Council).

[3] Report of the Quebec Merchants on the request of the Legislative Committee on Commerce, Jan. 5, 1787 ; C.O. 42/50.

[4] *Ibid.* The planters refer pointedly to this drain of specie in a " Report of the Committee appointed to enquire into the present state of the Intercourse between the British West Indies and His Majesty's Colonies in North America." Jamaica, Jan. 8, 1788, C.O. 137/87. It is also interesting to note that there was (from the West Indian point of view) the discouraging habit of referring to Canada the condemned contraband foreign spirits, free of the one shilling duty. *Ibid.*, C.O. 137/87.

Indies, an additional duty of 3*d.* per gallon on foreign molasses might be laid on, while the 6*d.* duty on British West India rum imported directly should be reduced to 3*d.*

The main problem which faced the Colonial Secretary was the expediency of prohibiting or restraining the importation of foreign molasses. It had long been the subject of conversations, and Adam Smith's wisdom had been culled to buttress the defences of both views.[1] The Government were in a quandary. If the molasses trade were restricted and distillation prohibited, the Indian trade would suffer. If duties were altered so as to cheapen the price of rum by a direct trade, the British carrying trade might lose, and the navigation laws suffer an affront. " Britain," declared Councillor William Grant on one occasion " holds her Colonies and Plantations merely with a commercial view. The representations of the Commercial Body will ever have due weight at home."[2] Unfortunately, on this occasion the administration faced a dilemma of their own making—a clash of interests within their own mercantilist scheme of things.

The man on whom these perplexing responsibilities chiefly fell was Thomas Townshend, Lord Sydney, who had become Pitt's Secretary of State for the Home Department in December, 1783. As a Chatham Whig, Townshend had been in opposition during the whole period of the North Ministry, reaping the reward of loyalty in 1782, when he became Secretary of War in Rockingham's second administration. On Shelburne's succession as Prime Minister, he took over the Home Office, and in this capacity he was nominally leader of the House of Commons from July, 1782, to April, 1783. His abilities were not first rate, and the real burden of the defence of the ministry during that hectic period fell upon Pitt.[3] Apparently, however, as a reward for his service in defending the peace he was granted a peerage, becoming Baron Sydney of Chislehurst in February, 1783.[4]

Sydney's real power in Colonial affairs is open to serious

[1] See a paper accompanying a memorial, June 12, 1787; C.O. 42/50.
[2] Council Minutes, April 27, 1784; C.O. 45/4.
[3] Stanhope, *Life of Pitt*, I, pp. 63, 82 (Edition of 1879).
[4] See Wraxall's *Memoirs*, II, p. 424.

question. Wraxall suggests that he owed his continuance in office to the fact that his daughter had married Pitt's elder brother, Lord Chatham. Whether this be true or not, judging from all contemporary report, Sydney appears to have exhibited little of his old vigour in the Lords, and one is inclined to think that behind the decisions which bore the signature of the Secretary of State there lay the influence of William Pitt.

Sydney proposed first of all to investigate the strong West Indian demands. On August 25, 1787, the Quebec Council were asked to consider a letter from the Colonial Secretary, which accompanied a summary of the West India complaints.[1] This time there was added the very genuine grievance that the rum trade was handicapped by the sale of liquor brought across the border from the American States.

The Governor, Lord Dorchester, was commanded to transmit an account of the number of distilleries established, with the quantity of spirits they were likely to distil. He was further asked to state whether rum of equal quality distilled in the province from foreign molasses, could be sold at a lower price than rum imported from the West India Islands either directly or through Great Britain; if sold at a lower price, in what proportion and to what causes such a proportion might be due; whether the inhabitants of Quebec or the Indians were likely to prefer the rum so distilled though of an inferior quality to the rum of the West India Islands; whether rum distilled from foreign molasses in the countries belonging to the United States was illicitly brought into the province of Quebec for the use of the inhabitants and Indians upon such terms as to interfere with the sale of the rum or spirits either distilled in Canada or imported from His Majesty's Islands, or from Great Britain; and finally whether rum imported into Quebec from the West Indies stood in need of any protection or encouragement to enable it to meet upon an equal footing rum distilled in the province or brought into it from the United States.

The basis of the report of the Committee of the whole Council both in attack and defence was the Indian trade.[2] On this

[1] Council Minutes, Aug. 25, 1787—in consideration of a report from Whitehall, dated May 28, 1787; C.O. 45/6.

[2] Report of Committee of Whole Council, Quebec, Wednesday, Nov. 7, 1787; C.O. 42/12, fol. 187; also Dorchester to Sydney, Que., Nov. 10, 1787 (enclosing report); C.O. 42/12, fol. 171.

occasion they determinedly opposed the prevention of the importation of foreign molasses either directly or by equalizing the duties. As for the suppression of distilleries, they considered it not only as prejudicial to the individuals engaged, but as " giving the most decided advantage to the American States in the fisheries and Indian trade."

From the point of view of the Canadian merchant, it was only this cheap product of foreign molasses which saved the fur trade from American competition and avoided the dangerous evil of smuggling. Owing to their proximity the American States had been able to reduce the cost of distilling to about one half that of the British colony.[1] So far the duty of only 4*d*. on foreign molasses rendered smuggling of no great occurrence. Nevertheless, that duty, plus the additional costs of freight and distillation, did enable the United States to supply the Indians and the fisheries at a lower rate than the British in Canada.[2] England with her new industrialism might maintain the lead in cheap manufactures, but she could not hope to continue to monopolize the fur trade in a country now declared to be American, if the Indians secured their rum at cheaper rates from American traders. The fact that Jamaica or other varieties of West Indian rum were of better quality and more potent than the home products of the United States or Canada made little appeal to the Indian or " habitant " who made little or no distinction between the two.[3]

Almost immediately, the Governor wrote to Sydney, enclosing his Council's report, and in his letter he summed up the conclusions of the investigation. In order to enable West Indian rum to meet on equal terms the rum distilled in the province, the duty of 6*d*. per gallon should be taken off and

[1] One gallon of molasses generally yielded one gallon of rum, and when of this uniform strength, it distilled for 3*d*. to 4*d*. a gallon, including 1*d*. the gallon for the casks if furnished by distillers ; C.O. 42/12, fol. 172.

[2] Rum distilled in the United States was actually sold at New York, Boston and Albany for 1*s*. 3*d*. a gallon, and West Indian rum for 2*s*., as compared with 2*s*. 3*d*. and 2*s*. 9*d*. in Canada. See Report of Jamaica Committee, C.O. 137/87.

[3] This was more generally true, since it had become the habit to reduce West Indian rum to the strength of home-made distilled rum by mixing it with water. According to Dorchester, Jamaica rum was often mixed in the proportion of 10 to 20 gallons of water to 100 gallons of rum, and other varieties in the proportion of 4 to 8 to the 100, to bring them down to the ordinary proof of rum distilled in the United States ; C.O. 42/12, fol. 172.

the supply of the West Indies with timber and provisions confined to Great Britain and her colonies. The Jamaica Committee's report had advocated the increase of the Molasses duty to one shilling. Dorchester on the contrary urged that in order to avoid smuggling and to prevent the supply of the fisheries and Indians by the Americans, the duty of 4*d.* per gallon on foreign molasses should be entirely abolished.

The first recommendation was not likely to be kindly received by shipping interests. It foretold the end of the triangular trade in so far as the popular commodity rum was concerned, and promised the promotion of a direct trade, which Canada would undoubtedly have difficulty in supporting. The second proposal was sure to meet with even less approval by West Indian interests. It was bound to revive the old antagonism between northern and southern colonies so apparent in the " Canada *v.* Guadaloupe " conflict of 1762. If free trade in foreign molasses meant increased progress in the fur trade and a surer grip of the fisheries, it also represented a real blow to the West Indian molasses and distilling industry. On the matter of the abolition of the 6*d.* duty, the West Indian interests were allied with the Canada merchants as opposed to the shipping interests who favoured the triangular trade. On the question of Canadian distilleries, cheap molasses and home-made rum, it became a contest between the ageing powers of the West Indian planters and the growing might of a merchant class, to whom, since the disastrous settlement of 1783, the fur trade and the fisheries had assumed even greater significance.

Sydney was apparently anxious to solve the problem on its merits, reacting neither to Dorchester's optimism nor to West Indian intimidation. It was a knotty question which had to be solved within the circle of the Navigation Laws, and he referred it, in its widest aspects, to the careful consideration of the new Board of Trade.[1] Had Pitt succeeded with his bill in 1784, Adam Smith's principles would have cleared the air, and a balance might have been sought in a general imperial reciprocity. But this situation was controlled by the spirit of the Enabling Acts which had succeeded one another ever since

[1] Minutes of Committee of Council of Trade, Whitehall, March 31, 1788, B.T. 5/5.

1783. Their spirit, as we have seen, was one of doctrinaire expediency—of compromising mercantilist theory with the needs of the situation, by methods in which monopolists pretended to believe, but went far to deny their own principles in carrying out.

Nevertheless, a new opinion was developing in contradiction to the dogmas of " a nation dominated by shop-keepers." Its progress was inevitably slow, for the roots of orthodoxy lay deep.[1] In the session of 1785, Pitt had made his last effort to carry a measure of Parliamentary reform, but leave even to discuss the bill in the House was refused. In 1779 North had failed with his Irish Relief bill against the monopolistic jealousies of the merchant class. Six years later Pitt faced the same problem, and he too failed. His proposals aimed at bringing Ireland entirely within the fold of the navigation system. But as usual, pressure of the trading classes compelled modifications—concessions to vested mercantile interests which robbed the bill of any value—and it was withdrawn. Dr. Johnson's words were not accurate, but they were expressive of a great deal in Adam Smith, " a few great families who had accumulated a vast amount of borough patronage, and a rich and corrupt mercantile class which had acquired by bribery an ascendancy in the chief towns, had got possession of the government of the country."

The project of a commercial treaty with France was originally an idea of Shelburne's, and mainly on his initiative the Treaty of 1783 contained an article whereby France and England agreed to nominate without delay commissioners to draw up a commercial treaty " on the basis of reciprocity and mutual convenience," to be completed not later than January, 1786.[2] Not until after a lapse of three years was Eden sent over to Paris to conduct the negotiations. The fruits of his efforts, the commercial treaty of 1786, may be taken as the first successful step in the scientific handling of England's economic relations with other powers.[3]

[1] Professor Clapham remarks that " there is no reason to think that at any time between 1783 and 1793, Pitt's Cabinet was ready to throw overboard the Navigation Code." *Cambridge History of British Foreign Policy*, Vol. I, p. 153.

[2] See Fitzmaurice, *Life of Shelburne*, Vol. III, pp. 166, 167, 318, 323, 386.

[3] According to Lecky it constitutes Pitt's chief title to legislative fame; Lecky, W. E. H., *History of England*, Vol. V (Ed. 1902), p. 307.

Despite the opposition of anti-French jingoists and die-hard monopolists, the treaty was carried in Parliament by two to one. Only the remarkable acquiescence of the commercial classes explains the phenomenon. It was becoming apparent that the new industrial giant demanded fresh markets which Ireland and the colonies could not supply; but most important of all, Board of Trade statistics revealed that England was to have the best of the bargain.

The treaty represented the first faint impress of Pitt's "new Toryism" on the adamantine block of the mercantile system. Only the French Revolution interrupted and wrecked a great beginning. The threads of that beginning were not again picked up until Huskisson's day, in the third decade of another century.

It is impossible to deduce what political influence here, and what vested interests there, help or retarded the formation of that fresh policy. Some seed of Shelburne's liberalism had taken root, and it is reasonable to suppose that the treaty did express the awakening of a new spirit, a new and less shackled condition of thought on commercial questions. Undoubtedly it made the way more smooth for the gradual reduction of the bars which hindered Canadian and American commerce,[1] and facilitated the solution of the perplexing problem of West Indian trade which confronted the Home Secretary so formidably.

The Board of Trade reported to Sydney on March 31, 1788.[2] They advocated a compromise in the form of a limited reciprocity. The *6d.* duty should be taken off all rum imported in vessels that should carry to the islands a cargo of lumber and provisions, or "having brought such rum to Canada, should load with a cargo of lumber and provisions and enter into bond for the landing of the same in the islands under proper regulations."

In June of 1788 this first modification of the Quebec Revenue Act was passed into law. It was entitled "an Act to allow the importation of rum or other spirits from British Colonies or

[1] See Chap. VI.

[2] Minutes of the Committee of Council of Trade, Whitehall, March 31, 1788; (Brit. Mus.) Add. MS. 38391, fol. 356; also B.T. 5/5.

Plantations in the West Indies, into Quebec without payment of duty under certain restrictions."[1] It carried into effect almost completely the recommendations of the Committee of the Board of Trade. Vessels carrying cargoes of lumber, provisions, horses or cattle were permitted to import into the province, free of any duty, rum " of value equal to that of the outward cargo already carried or engaged under proper security to be carried." In order to adjust the values of exchange, a rating schedule was attached. Thus a ton of flour rated at £13 a ton should be entitled to an import of a hogshead or 100 gallons of rum free of duty, and similar ratings applied to staves, hoops and provisions.[2]

Yet, after all, the bill was but a half-way measure to stimulate Canadian industry rather than a definite settlement of West Indian grievances. If there were victory for either side, it fell to the Canada merchants. But the laurels were few. The foreign molasses trade was left severely alone, and West Indian rum was given only a limited opportunity to compete with the Quebec distillery industry. In other words, the triangular trade was hardly affected, because the exports of lumber and provisions from Canada could pay for but a tiny share of the rum which Canada required above her own home manufacture.[3] The Act was a grudging aid to Canadian agriculture and the lumber trade, but as an offering to the West Indian rum and molasses interest, it was altogether meagre.

The Canada merchants lost no time in petitioning for an amendment. The decline of the West Indian energies was never more clearly evident than in the earnest attempt of the Canadian interests to manœuvre an extension, whilst the Island representatives at the New York Tavern stood almost silently apart.

The merchants admitted that there had been a large export of lumber during 1789, as compared with the meagre cargoes of

[1] Passed June 10; Royal Assent, June 25, 1788; 28 Geo. III, c. 39; *Lords' Journals*, XXXVIII; MacPherson, *op. cit.*, IV, p. 173.

[2] This schedule was arranged on the advice of Thomas Irving, Commissioner of Customs, who was requested by George Chalmers, Chief Clerk of the Committee of the Privy Council to state his opinion on the proposed amendment of the New Revenue Act; C.O. 42/12, fol. 271.

[3] " There was so great a disproportion between the value of the Canadian cargoes and the West India cargoes in return, that the exemption would have little and partial effect "; Report (unsigned) to Grenville on the trade of Canada; London, Nov. 4, 1789, C.O. 42/66.

1788,[1] but a regulation which cramped trade to a pendulum-like " to and fro " motion was handicapping even those who had undoubtedly most to gain from it. No cargo of the enumerated Canadian articles was of sufficient value to purchase an exemption of duty for more than one half a cargo of rum.[2] They fully realized the value of the triangular trade to Great Britain. " The circuitous voyage has been held up as an advantage to the navigation of the Kingdom on the principle that the more voyages made, the greater will be the number of ships and sailors employed."[3] But under their suggested amendment, which called for an increased direct trade, the triangular system would ultimately benefit, through the greater prosperity of Canada and her consequent increased capacity as a purchaser of British manufactures.[4]

In essence the merchants' petition was a request for the continuation of a reciprocity, as under the Act of 1788, but with one alteration. Instead of restricting the trade in value to a balance of cargoes on one voyage, the reciprocity should be assessed on a total number of voyages for a single company or individual. This would relieve the disproportion which was inevitable under a system of direct exchange, whereby a bulky low-priced freight was traded for a compact and comparatively expensive cargo of rum.[5]

The petition was submitted to the new Colonial Secretary, W. W. Grenville,[6] on January 23, 1790, along with a letter from Dorchester, in comment. The governor was apparently perplexed in his own mind by the dilemma. He appreciated

[1] Observations submitted to the consideration of the Committee of Council appointed by Lord Dorchester to make enquiry concerning the effect of the alterations desired by a memorial of the merchants concerned on the Export Trade; submitted Jan. 3, 1790; C.O. 45/11, fol. 163.

[2] Memorial of Merchants engaged in Export trade, Proprietors of Mills, Flour Manufacturers, Bakers, Coopers, etc. Dec. 9, 1789; C.O. 45/11, fol. 94 and C.O. 42/12, fol. 657.

[3] C.O. 45/11, fol. 165.

[4] " Under the present laws, 25,000 ton of shipping sails from London to Jamaica in Ballast,—from Jamaica to London with a freight,—from London to Quebec with a freight. Under the amendment 9000 of shipping must sail from London to Quebec with a freight to as many ships as the Imports of Canada can employ, and the rest in ballast. From Quebec to Jamaica with a freight and from Jamaica to Quebec with a freight to the amount of tonnage of rum imported " ; C.O. 45/11, fol. 169.

[5] Petition of Merchants signed by 68 principal citizens, Dec. 9, 1789; C.O. 45/11, fols. 94–5.

[6] Grenville succeeded Sydney as Secretary of State in June, 1789.

the benevolent intentions of the Act of 1788, but realized its insufficiency. He saw the value in a natural balance of trade which the merchants' suggestions would bring about, but he feared that such an amendment would discourage the triangular route.[1]

Furthermore, he was beginning to experience the qualms which Thomas Irving had unreasonably felt with regard to the late measure. The Commissioner of Customs had advised the Board of Trade at the time that even so limited a reciprocity would sink an annual revenue of £6000. Such a sum, declared Irving, " would have to be made up, for besides the 6*d.* a gallon lost on rum, the duty of 3*d.* a gallon on molasses applied to provincial purposes and 1*d.* a gallon paid to the British Exchequer would be given up, because the plan would in great measure put a stop to the importation of molasses."[2] Irving had obviously exaggerated the extent and importance of the reciprocity. Yet if the merchants' suggested amendments were carried into effect, might there not be a danger of the total annihilation of the revenue of the provinces,[3] " more especially on considering the Act of Parliament of the 18th of His present Majesty relative to future taxations on the colonies " ?

This measure, to which Dorchester so timorously referred, was known as " the Colonial Tax Repeal Act " and had been passed in a belated mood of conciliation by the North Government in 1778. North explains its immense significance in one of the last of his official despatches to Haldimand.[4] Referring to the oath which required all applicants for land to acknowledge the King to be the Supreme Legislature of the province, he added, " I think it necessary to observe to you that the Declaration however general cannot extend to Taxation, *Parliament having by the 18th of His Present Majesty, and in the most express terms restrained itself from ever imposing any Taxes or Duties in the Colonies except for the Regulation of Trade, the product of which Taxes and Duties to be disposed of by the Provincial Assemblies.*" There was a basis for doubt in Dor-

[1] Letter of Dorchester to Nepean, considered at Whitehall. Minutes of Committee of Trade, Aug. 4, 1790 ; (Brit. Mus.) Add. MS. 38392, fol. 140b.

[2] Whitehall, April 7, 1788 ; C.O. 42/12, fol. 271.

[3] C.O. 42/12, fol. 663.

[4] North to Haldimand, Whitehall, July 24, 1783 ; C.O. 45/11, fol. 79.

chester's question, for England had thus specifically declared that she would not tax except by regulation of trade, and increased reciprocity implied less regulation.[1] If governmental control through the mercantile system were abandoned, the road was dangerously open to imported varieties of American self-government.

Grenville took a serious view of the merchants' petition. The provisions of the Canada Bill of 1791 were already being formulated. Nevertheless, late in December of 1789, he referred to the consideration of the Quebec Council a most important questionnaire.[2] The fact that a document of this type was sent out from the Colonial Office goes far to indicate the leavening spirit at work in England's mercantilist conscience. Orthodoxy was being assailed by doubts and in danger of attack by those of its own adherents who were willing to test its efficiency by examination.

There were three main problems which were put up for discussion: Will the Trade and Navigation of the Empire gain or lose by alterations? How will they operate on the interests of West Indian planters? What diminution in revenue under the Quebec Revenue Act (14 Geo. III, c. 88) may be expected?

The report of the private Committee of the Legislative Council may be taken as a fair criticism of the whole system of triangular trade. It was an appeal to the new and expanding industrial England, as against the old mercantilist caste of vested interests. In 1790 the real clash in colonial evaluations became fully apparent. Territorial possessions as potential market zones were now vastly increasing in importance over tropical islands of supply. Even the Navigation Laws were in increasing danger of modification as a result of this ardently developing faith in industrial progress with its new interpretation of colonial worth.

In answer to official doubts as to the effect of modifications on the Navigation System, the Committee were able to reply that, "Whatever creates Manufactures must necessarily increase the Trade of the Nation, and whatever increases the

[1] Of course the Government retained independently the much disputed Crown, Territorial and Casual Revenues, and other royal dues of the "old *regime*."

[2] C.O. 45/11, ff. 75–95.

Trade of the Nation must eventually increase its Navigation.' As for the West Indian planters, they would obviously be gainers by the amendments proposed, for freer trade would bring an additional quantity of provisions and lumber to market and would eventually increase the Canadian export of their produce.

The Committee were thus emphasizing the benefits accruing to the triangular trade viewed as a commercially productive system. Heretofore ships sailing direct from Britain to the West Indies went there chiefly in ballast, relying on great homeward freights. If, on the contrary, British shippers could obtain first, freight to Quebec in British manufactures, salt, wines and rum, secondly, freight from Quebec to the Islands in flour, biscuit, fish and lumber, and thirdly, freight from the Islands home to Britain, in rum, sugar and other West Indian produce, both planters and carriers would be gainers by the circuitous route. If, on the other hand, British ships returned from the Islands to Quebec, their voyages and freights would be multiplied, and a new carrying trade would be opened to Britain by a similarly triangular roundabout route. "Canada's northern situation," they added, "shuts it out eternally from maritime competition, and in this, as in other respects, attaches it permanently to the British Empire."

As for the problem of a diminished revenue, in the opinion of the whole Council it was one which the creators of the Revenue Act of 1774 could solve for themselves. "If that power in its wisdom thinks proper to encourage the commerce of the infant colony by opening its way to the most profitable markets, it will also, when requisite constitutionally, call upon this Colony for such aids and supplies as are consistent and proportionate to its wealth. . . . So soon as it shall be found wise (and the Committee hope the day is not distant) to consolidate the strength and union of all His Majesty's North American Dominions by a system of government analogous to that on which they depend for their existence, this Colony will not be backward in finding the means of relieving the Parent state from a part of that burden which she has so long and patiently borne."[1]

[1] In the meantime as an alternative source of revenue, the Committee of Council suggested that an Import or Excise Tax on the Rum consumed in the

Only to a degree did Pitt's Act of 1791 answer that challenge. The Government were too deeply entangled with the issue of the Canada Bill, and later on too oppressed with the responsibilities of a French war to give proper consideration to so thorough and comprehensive a document. Renewed petitions by merchants met with the reply that all consideration of West India trade relations would be postponed until the institution of the new Act, wherein substitute duties for revenue might be contemplated. As for West India preferential treatment, it was a subject for mutual arrangement, and a decision could only be taken after further reference to the Islands.[1]

But the Canada Act of 1791 made no attempt to solve the difficulty.[2] Clause XLVI recited the Colonial Tax Repeal Act of 1778, but hastened to declare that nothing in that repeal could prevent the operation of any Act of Parliament establishing Prohibitions or imposing duties for the Regulation of Navigation and Commerce.[3]

province would produce a revenue, at 3*d*. per gallon, vastly greater than that which the Amendments (proposed to the Act of 1788) would take away. Authorised statistics revealed that the duties paid in to the Treasury since May 1, 1783, totalled £27,411 2*s*. 4*d*. sterling, making an annual average of £3915 17*s*. 6*d*. Of this sum only £8,686 11*s*. 3*d*. had been produced from West Indian rum. It was further estimated that the annual average would have been reduced to £1337 1*s*. 6*d*. had the Act of 1788 not been passed. (See Appendix B.) The remainder of the revenue had been collected from molasses, British and foreign brandies and rum brought coastwise. The revenue, therefore, would only be lessened £1200 to £1300 by granting the merchants' request, whereas an Excise of 3*d*. per gallon on spirits collected by the Provincial Legislature would amount to upwards of £5000. To this could be added the duty on foreign molasses and spirits retained under the Quebec Revenue Act: "Thus," concluded the report, "the British Treasury would fix relief in the whole to the amount of about £7500 per annum, without injury to the Trade and navigation of the Empire, or immediate interests of the province." The report was signed by George Pownall, the Chairman, and unanimously accepted by the whole Council. C.O. 45/11, fol. 79.

[1] Whitehall, May 24, 1791. Reply to letter from Mr. Bernard transmitting petition of Merchants, referring to former application of Dec. 9, 1789, and Dorchester's letter, and praying amendments in Acts, 28 Geo. III, c. 6 and 39; (Brit. Mus.) Add. MS. 38393, fol. 84b.

[2] Dundas to Dorchester, Whitehall, Sept. 16, 1791. Referring to the Canada Bill of 1791, Dundas concludes: "By the Act of last session the duties payable to His Majesty under the Act of the 14th of His Majesty's Reign, Chap. 88, on Articles imported into the Province of Quebec are suffered to remain upon their former footing; but I have it in Command to intimate to your Lordship that as soon as the Legislatures of the Provinces of Upper Canada and Lower Canada shall have passed Laws laying the same or other Duties to an equal amount to those which become payable under the Acts, and such Act shall have obtained the Royal Assent, His Majesty's Ministers will be ready to propose to Parliament a Repeal of the Act above mentioned"; Shortt and Doughty, *op. cit.*, II, p. 1030.

[3] *Ibid.*, p. 1050.

As a result the main features of the Quebec Revenue Act with its fiscal advantages and its discriminations in favour of the triangular trade remained unchanged. The long agitations of Canada merchant and West India planter had produced minor relaxations, but governance through the Navigation System had been fundamentally little affected by the perceptible spirit of reform. Not until the days of Huskisson was Monopoly to bow the knee to Reciprocity. Meanwhile, mercantile interests fortified themselves for a time longer on the bed-rock of dogma and empiricism. Only persistent realities which, like the French commercial Treaty of 1786, pointed to concrete benefits, secured any modifications of an imperial system. Defence, said Adam Smith, was more important than opulence, and the accomplishment of both in the opinion of eighteenth-century Britain largely depended on the triangular trade. Such being the case, the many hours which the Board of Trade and the Secretaries of State expended in deciding the proper manner of taxing or transporting rum is not extraordinary. The Navigation Laws were the product of their age, and rum in the eighteenth century was made to play no small part in furthering the ends of that in most ways artificial system. Rum helped to retain the Canadian fur trade, secured the fisheries, and increased British shipping by means of the triangular trade. In so doing it contributed to the avowed object of the Navigation Laws, "the augmentation of British sea power."

CHAPTER VII

THE SEARCH FOR NAVAL STORES

WHILE the problem of trade relations between the West Indies and Canada claimed the efforts and attention of a nation whose theories of empire were still based on mercantilist conceptions of sea power and monopoly, the northern colony began to acquire an even more direct significance within the Navigation System. Furs and fish, of course, remained the staple articles of export. So long as West Indian rum could be supplied cheaply, and the boundary terms of the Treaty of 1783 be neglected diplomatically, their profits were regular and assured. On the other hand, as an importer of British manufactures it was inevitable that the country could supply but limited market facilities for some time to come. This was true not because of any growing local competition, but merely on account of the undeveloped wants of the colony.[1] Cheap merchandise, blankets, trinkets, powder and articles of clothing were still required in quantity for the Indian trade, but the possibilities of a great immediate expansion were few.

What gave Canada most immediate prominence in the official limelight was the crying demand for naval stores.[2] During this whole period, the Colonial Office was much more concerned with what the colony could supply than what she might accept. The consequences of a decrepit Navy, the result of shaky dependence on European sources of supply, had been

[1] The value of British manufactures yearly exported to Canada, Nova Scotia and Newfoundland on an average of six years, ending 1774, was £310,916
On an average of six years since the war, ending 1789 ... £603,928
To the British West Indies, for same period before the war £1,182,379
To the British West Indies, for same period since the war . £1,297,275
Original Correspondence, Board of Trade, 1777–1807; C.O. 5/2.

[2] After the Seven Years' War, there was a grave shortage of seasoned timber, sails, rigging and cordage. Lord Egmont, the First Lord of the Admiralty, presented the necessity for a large expenditure on the Navy, but Grenville, on the plea of economy, refused to take action. See Hunt, William, *Political History of England*, Vol. X, p. 53.

brought perilously home during the war.[1] The American Revolution had resulted in some severe humiliations to British naval prestige and the memory of those humiliations was particularly vivid and particularly painful.

Heretofore the Baltic countries had been the chief sources of British naval stores. During the whole of the eighteenth century England's navy had been mainly supplied by Russia, Norway, Denmark, Poland and Sweden.[2] In fact, almost all the hemp and no small part of the timber supply came from Russian territories alone.[3] In consequence, both the supply and the price of these commodities were apt to be regulated by the humours of the Empress, who occasionally found amusement in hostile prohibitions or friendly speculations. At one time the watchful Catherine had managed to obtain a " corner " on hemp, which raised the price to British merchants 40 per cent.[4]

This dependence on foreign supply had begun at an early date. Even in Tudor times the scarcity of lumber was felt, and by the end of the seventeenth century there was an almost total reliance on the Continent.[5] From Danzig, Sweden, Denmark, Norway, Germany and Russia came masts, planks, staves and boards.[6] A great portion of ordinary timber was used as fuel for the iron industry, but increasingly with the expansion of British sea power, the supply went mainly to the construction of ships. In the first decade of George I's reign,

[1] See Chapter III, p. 38.

[2] In 1779 England imported from Baltic countries 2739 masts and spars; France, 1968; Holland, 3425. *Barham Papers*, Vol. II, p. 220.

[3] Board of Trade, Commercial; C.O. 390/9.

Josiah Tucker, *Tracts*, Answers to Objections. No. V, p. 32.

[4] See Report (unsigned) to Grenville on the Trade to Canada, with arguments in favour of bounties, Nov. 4, 1789; C.O. 42/66.

[5] Beer, G. L., *op. cit.*, p. 98.

Also Clapham, J. H., *An Economic History of Modern Britain*. In his introduction to the section on the Early Railway Age (1820–50) Professor Clapham remarks that England, unlike every continental country, had been stripped almost completely of its native woodland. " The ancient royal forests had been so neglected during the 18th century, and so heavily drawn upon for ships, timber and fuel during the wars, that in all probability they were emptier of serviceable trees in 1815 than at any time in their history. The New Forest had produced little fine timber since early Stuart times. A survey of 1608 had registered 123,927 trees then fit for navy use, a survey of 1707 could report only 12,476. In spite of forest legislation under William III and again in 1769 and 1770, there had been no recovery by 1793."

[6] See George, Joshua, *Trade and Navigation of Great Britain considered*, 3rd edition, London, 1731.

legal provision was made for the importation of all kinds of timber into England from the colonies free of duty,[1] and this preference was continued with the addition of bounties until the interruption of the American Revolution.

In Canada the French had pursued the policy of granting lands with specific reservations in the title deeds that all oak and pine timber should be kept for the king's use, until demanded by naval officials who were permitted to take what they desired without paying for it.[2] The new British policy altered the whole system of concessions, for the Governor was instructed to make no grant of timber lands at all, but to see that these were retained as royal reservations. The instructions to Governors Murray, Carleton and Haldimand express almost identically the desire that the Colony should furnish white pines " fit for masting our Royal Navy," and that lands on which there is any considerable growth and which are convenient for water carriage should be set apart as royal preserves.[3]

Until the influx of the Loyalists this policy was carried out with some success. The wilderness country to the west and south of the St. Lawrence gave the Navy Board every opportunity to make reservations unhampered by private property claims.[4] Extensive tracts of Crown lands were partitioned with the understanding that licences were to be given for the cutting of timber for naval purposes. Reservations were also made of all great pines on lands already granted, a measure

[1] 8 Geo. I, c. 12.

[2] Munro, W. B., *The Seigniorial System in Canada* (Harvard Historical Studies, Vol. XIII), pp. 74 and 195. See also Lower, A. R. M., " The Forest in New France," *Canadian Hist. Assoc. Report*, 1928.

[3] See C.O. 42/2 (No. 39), fol. 257 for Carleton's Instructions of Dec. 22, 1774, and No. 40 for Haldimand's Instructions of April 13, 1778. This letter also included an instruction for the preservation of an ironworks at St. Maurice.

[4] *Acts of Privy Council, Col.*, V, p. 230.

Dated Feb. 20, 1769, is an order in accordance with the Committee Report of 28th January advising that "the Treasury do take such measures as expedient to cause inspection of lands not private property in Quebec and that part of New York lying on Lake Champlain, as likewise within New Hampshire and New York, between the Connecticut River and the Hudson, and Nova Scotia which lies to the North of the Bay of Fundy. The Lord Commissioners of the Treasury are to give directions for surveys of white pine growth, the advantages and disadvantages of export from thence. They are also to submit to the Council what further measures may be taken to preserve white pine trees in America, and secure a perpetual supply of masts and other naval stores for the use of the Royal Navy." C.O. 42/28, Pt. II.

subject to considerable vocal comment on the part of the French owners.

In 1768 Francis MacKay wrote to Lord Hillsborough that he had surveyed part of Lake Champlain and marked 500 red pines and cypress masts for the Navy, some of them ten feet in circumference, and 100 white pine masts some twelve feet in circumference, and had continued to mark trees for the Navy "notwithstanding the public clamour of those who hold the French King's grants which reserved 'bois de construction,' about the interpretation of which there is a difference of opinion."[1]

Following the war the despairing reports of Sandwich's administration, and the dwindling numerical powers of the English Navy were proof sufficient of the urgent need for renewed action. "The safety of the state is most intimately connected," said William Knox, with "the provision of timber for the construction of ships of the line."[2] The "Broad Arrow" policy had been pursued actively, and with some success in New England. It became the Admiralty's aim to apply it with equal vigour in Canada, Nova Scotia[3] and New Brunswick.

Carleton had declared his belief in the future of a Canadian timber trade and the possibilities of a thriving ship-building industry.[4] Sheffield had referred to the need of the West Indies for Canadian staves and lumber, and the advantage of bounties to encourage that trade—adding in conclusion that "the lumber of those Colonies is the best in America, the oak of Canada is heavier and much more lasting than that of New England," and "no part of the world furnishes greater advantages for shipbuilding."[5] Sheffield's views would have been less significant had they not represented the opinions of men who claimed first-hand knowledge. In spite of the fact that the Treaty of 1783 had cut off the Lake Champlain and Vermont region, Attorney-General Monk claimed that "Canadian oak is far superior to any other in North America, particularly

[1] C.O. 42/28, Pt. II.

[2] *Extra Official State Papers*, p. 40.

[3] The system of marking masting trees with a "Broad Arrow" had been in vogue in Nova Scotia since 1721, so that little of value was left in Nova Scotia proper. See Albion, *Forests and Sea Power*, pp. 352-3.

[4] Whitehall, March 16, 1784; B.T. 5/1.

[5] Sheffield, *op. cit.*, p. 83.

around the St. Lawrence in the neighbourhood of St. Regis." It was better than that of Lake Champlain and for ships, tougher and harder. The Lake oak timber he advised would be best for staves.[1]

As a consequence of such encouraging reports, the Lieutenant Governor[2] was supplied in 1785 with additional instructions regarding timber reservations in the neighbourhood (presumably north) of Lake Champlain, and between that Lake and the River St. Lawrence. Easy water carriage was a necessary accessory, care was to be taken to prevent wastage and no saw mills were to be erected without a Government licence.[3]

Despite all the encouragements which reservations and minor bounty preferences provided,[4] Admiralty minutes of transactions continued to record disappointment, just as reports from Canadian correspondents continued to reflect boundless hope. That Canada oak did not compare with New England or European becomes apparent from final Reports of the Admiralty Advisory Committee. The best oak for shipbuilding grew on the banks of Lake Champlain which had been granted to America by treaty.[5] The fact that this territory belonging to Vermont, was beyond the boundary line of Quebec Province, inspired the efforts of Levi and Ethan Allan to secure their natural market by way of the Richelieu and St. Lawrence through British territory. The free admission of naval stores by a proclamation of April 18, 1787, was the fruits of their bargaining, Carleton's recognition of Canada's insufficiency,

[1] A letter from James Monk, June 6, 1786, quoted by a Mr. Manchut; (Brit. Mus.) Add. MS. 38346, ff. 359–60.

[2] Following Haldimand's resignation in 1784, two Lieutenant-Governors, Hamilton and Hope, succeeded each other until the return of Carleton, now Lord Dorchester, in 1786.

[3] B.T. 6/102, No. 53.

[4] In 1786 a bill was passed to continue the laws relating to giving encouragement to the importation of naval stores from the British Colonies in America. *Lords' Journals*, XXXVII, p. 522b.

Bounties on the importation of oak, timber and staves had expired some years previous (1775). The London merchants in their petition and report of Feb. 8, 1786, prayed for a renewal. Only slowly (as compared with hemp bounties) were forms of encouragement initiated. See C.O. 42/49, *passim*. Strangely enough, not until 1796 was naval timber permitted to be imported duty free from the North American Colonies. *Lords' Journals*, XXXVII, 522b.

[5] B.T. 5/1. See also Silas Deane's suggestion for a canal to facilitate the introduction into Vermont of timber and masts for the Navy. Deane to Dorchester, Oct. 25, 1785; C.O. 42/66.

and the Admiralty's pressing demands for oak planks and white pine masts.[1]

As for Canada's immediate prospects—she remained, in the words of her advocates, a "land of opportunity," but no more. Shipbuilding existed as a minor industry, while staves, clap boards and timber of sorts found limited vent in the West Indies and Newfoundland;[2] but the United States continued to be the main source of supply for the Islands as well as an important supplement to Britain's naval resources. The Revolution had done little to alter the American trade in natural products, and naval stores coming to Britain in either American or British ships were received as if America were still a British colony.[3] But it is little wonder, considering the extreme cost of freightage across the Atlantic, that the dependence on continental sources, particularly Russian, continued.[4] Not until the early nineteenth century did Canada come into real prominence as a timber land. Up to that time, with the exception of some few gallons of spruce beer,[5] three or four cargoes of masts was the annual export, and these appear to have been chiefly the product of the "broad arrow" in New Brunswick.[6]

[1] Even prior to the proclamation the merchants of Montreal reported on Jan. 23, 1787, that "the most valuable part of our lumber comes at present from Vermont and must be profitable to this country for ship building and exportations, yielding also a gain on the expenses and on the goods given in exchange." Nevertheless they advocated bounties on shipbuilding timber to counteract the Vermont trade and on white oak and red oak staves. C.O. 42/50.

[2] The supply to Newfoundland, like that to the West Indies, was small. In 1785 there were two cargoes from Canada and one from Nova Scotia and the trade did not greatly increase. Report of Richard Routh, Collector of Customs, Dec. 23, 1785; B.T. 5/2, fol. 365.

[3] Clapham, J. H., in *Cambridge History of British Foreign Policy*, I, 153.

[4] See Edward Long, *op. cit.*, (1784) for a comparison of the Canadian and Nova Scotian with the American supply to the West Indies; (Brit. Mus.) Add. MS. 18274; also Ainslee, *Evidence from Custom's House Records;* B.T. 5/1, fol. 87. (Ainslee was obviously handling his evidence to support the Canada merchants' demand for freer West India trade, and it is liable to be exaggerated.)

[5] Treasury accounts include occasional references to Admiralty correspondence regarding "essence of spruce," from Quebec—"which, when brewed into beer may be of great service to the navy in preserving the seamen from scurvy." Treasury I, fol. 497. An indication of the demand for spruce beer in England is provided by a table for the years 1779 to 1781:

1779	4753 gallons.
1780	3562 ,,
1781	18496 ,,

(Brit. Mus.) Add. MS. 8133 B., fol. 280.

[6] Albion, *op. cit.*, p. 353.

If the whims of Baltic countries made the trade in timber a matter of serious speculation and worry, they similarly rendered the shortage of hemp and flax a subject of most grave concern. The cables which anchored British ships and the cordage and rigging which net-worked British masts were made from hemp, and the sails from the fibre of long flax. For both these articles, as has been noted, England relied upon Russia. Anderson claims that in one year £1,000,000 was expended on hemp and flax imported from St. Petersburg,[1] and on an average, half that amount yearly was spent on flax. Such an expenditure is sufficient to explain the anxiety to which such absolute dependence gave rise.[2]

In 1790 Britain imported over a million planks, about 90,000 boards and 1500 masts; *Colonial Policy of Great Britain considered*, etc., 1816.

A commentary on the Empire's failure to supply England's Navy with oak in the latter quarter of the eighteenth century is contained in a *Times'* leader of Friday, Aug. 17, 1928. "It will surprise many," says the writer, "to learn that Great Britain annually spends more than £2,000,000 on imports of oak and that less than one per cent of the supplies of that typically British timber is from the Empire, while three-quarters are grown in the United States."

In *The Times* of March 22, 1929, Lord Londonderry recalled the fact that in 1927 the value of timber imports into Britain amounted to £50,000,000, and that of this large sum no less than 90 per cent was paid to foreign sources.

[1] Board of Trade Report (Evidence), Court of St. James, Aug. 23, 1786. Edward Forster and Godfrey Thornton on behalf of the Russia Co. gave evidence to the effect that Russia supplied practically all the hemp and flax. With the exception of a trifling quantity from Prussia almost the entire quantity came from the same source. B.T. 5/4; also Anderson, *op. cit.*, Vol. III, p. 223.

[2] The Board of Trade compiled a list of foreign articles used in building and fitting a ship of 800 tons with the quantities and amount of duties thereon:

	Quantity.	*Duty.* £	s.	d.
Dantzig Oak Plank	10 loads	9	18	0
Dantzig Fir Deals (various sizes) ...	480 in number	20	0	0
Norway Fir Deals	200 in number	2	15	0
Memel Timber	29 loads	5	19	8
Swedish Iron	10 tons	28	1	0
Russian Iron	8 tons	27	18	0
Russian Tar	14 brls.	0	14	5
Russian Pitch	48 cwt.	1	19	7
Italy Brimstone	6 cwt.	1	19	7
Russian Hemp	44 tons	161	6	8
New England masts (7-ft. in circum.) ...	4 in number			
Riga masts (4-ft. in circum.)	4 in number			
Riga „ (4.6-ft. „)	4 in number	7	18	5
Riga „ (3-ft. „)	7 in number			
Norway „ (3-ft. „)	5 in number			
(2.6-ft. „)	20 in number			
(2-ft. „)	10 in number	4	19	0
(0.6-ft. „)	12 in number	0	13	2

B.T. 6/96 (1786).

In 1779 the Navy had been forced to take from depleted resources 9,000 tons of hemp, and by 1781 the consumption had reached the alarming figure of 12,000 tons.[1] In this extremity the matter was brought before the Cabinet, who considered every means of purchasing the stores at St. Petersburg and Riga. But English diplomatists found the task too formidable and it was abandoned.[2]

Every conceivable scheme of adding to the supply or securing substitutes was eagerly investigated and thoroughly discussed. It is amazing to note the avidity with which the Board of Trade clutched at possible methods of preparing hemp as a substitute for flax. "The discovery," read one report, "if found to answer that end, would certainly be at this particular juncture a matter of considerable and great national advantage and deserve every possible attention."[3] Later on, at the request of the Board of Trade, the Society for the Encouragement of Arts and Commerce attempted experiments with China hemp, even though it was proved that the variety would cost one-third more than Riga hemp to manufacture.[4]

In the manner of drowning men clutching at straws, the Parliament of 1781 pushed through a bill permitting the importation of flax into either England or Ireland "in any vessel belonging to any state in amity with His Majesty navigated by foreigners during the present hostilities."[5] At the same time the bounty Acts of 1767 and 1770 were extended,

[1] Chas. Middleton to Pitt, Aug. 26, 1786; *Letters and Papers of Charles, Lord Barham,* 1758–1813, Vol. II, p. 220.

The following table gives an account of the duties received on naval stores, mainly Russian, for the years 1779, 1780 and 1781:—

	1779.	*1780.*	*1781.*
Cordage	£45 3 2	£74 5 4	£42 13 0
Flax, Rough ...	Free	Free	Free
Hemp, Rough ...	£84,699 14 9	£61,822 3 6	£70,658 5 4
Iron Bar ...	£85,849 5 2	£84,357 19 9	£129,739 14 8
Oak Plank ...	£4,795 14 3	£2,650 3 2	£6,326 13 9
Timber, Fir ...	£12,742 9 5	£11,907 14 5	£11,541 18 2

Further statistics of duties reveal the huge sums spent on pitch, tar, saltpetre, tallow, turpentine, anchor stocks, bow sprits, deals, masts and knees. (Brit. Mus.) Add. MS. 8133 B, ff. 177–9.

[2] Chas. Middleton to Pitt, Aug. 26, 1786; *Ibid.*

[3] (Brit. Mus.) Add. MS. 14035; representation to the King relative to the discovery in the preparation of hemp, addressed to Viscount Stormont, Whitehall, June 12, 1781.

[4] Board of Trade, Nov. 17, 1786; B.T. 5/4, fols. 80, 82 and 88.

[5] *Lords' Journals,* Vol. XXXVI, 268a.

and the Board of Trade were given the supervision of £15,000 a year for the encouragement of the growth of hemp and flax in England.[1] To the Clerks of the Peace in all the counties were sent circular letters, enclosing copies of a pamphlet entitled *Directions for Raising Flax,* as well as a copy of the Act which listed the bounties.[2] At the first Quarter Sessions these were to be laid before the Justices of the Peace, who were to disperse information and consider the claims for bounties.

The returns of the Justices would seem to indicate that on a limited scale, the scheme of home cultivation bore fruit, and bounties were dispersed with easy regularity at yearly midsummer sessions.[3] The Isle of Ely provided the best returns for hemp, with Lincolnshire and Norfolk second, while Yorkshire and Lincolnshire appear to have been most suitable for flax.[4] Ireland did not come immediately under the scheme, although, not long after, the Lord-Lieutenant was able to report that the object "hemp culture was not only attainable," but "might be most advantageous to Ireland."[5]

From the time of Charles II, governors had spoken of the especial fitness of the soil and climate in the colonies for the production of these commodities. Yet all efforts to establish the industry appear to have been futile. At one time there had been a bounty of £8 per ton, which added to the duty paid on Russian hemp of £3 6*s.* 8*d.* gave a more than average preference.[6] Yet all such stimuli were of no avail.[7] Franklin asked rather sardonically, "Did ever any North American bring his hemp to England for this bounty? We have not yet

[1] *Ibid.*; 21 Geo. III, c. 58.

[2] Index 8373, *Journal*, p. 324, Entry 2, Bundle A (Dec. 21, 1781); also C.O. 391/88, fol. 325.

[3] Minutes of claims by Justices of the Peace at Midsummer Sessions, 1784; *Commons' Journals*, XL, p. 423.

[4] Total amount of hemp at 3*d.* per stone by Midsummer, 1784, 30,761½ stones.

Total amount of flax at 4*d.* per stone by Midsummer, 1784, 106,828 stones.

Total bounties, £2,164 19*s.* 8*d.*

Board of Trade Report, B.T. 5/2, fol. 263.

[5] B.T. 5/4, fols. 392 and 394.

In 1779 a bounty had been granted for the importation of flax and hemp from Ireland, but with little result. Anderson, *op. cit.*, IV, p. 261.

[6] Report to Grenville on the Trade to Canada, Nov. 4, 1789; C.O. 42/66.

[7] See (Brit. Mus.) Add. MS. 8133 B, fol. 141, for an account of bounties paid on hemp and flax and wood imported from America. The total for hemp and flax during the years 1771–5 was only £87 13*s.* 9¾*d.*

enough for our own consumption."[1] Sheffield observed that "Although an article of exportation from America, she does not raise a fiftieth part of her consumption."[2] Nevertheless, under the increasing urge of necessity England continued to lavish bounties and premiums down to the beginning of the American Revolution.[3]

American Independence coupled with the disasters to British sea power turned Britain's eyes definitely in the direction of Canada. The prospect, to the eager eyes of the Board of Trade, seemed hopeful. Considerable amounts had been grown under the easy efforts of the French government, and conditions of cultivation generally seemed very similar to those of Russia. The soil was good, but, as in the case of grain crops, war had retarded husbandry and farming methods remained old-fashioned. Only 5 or 6 bushels had been reaped from each bushel sown instead of 12 or 15.[4]

It has been noticed in a previous chapter that the Government were not slow in turning their energies to the encouragement of agriculture. In the case of the hemp, the new Board of Trade with incredible zest recommended that instructions be sent to the Governors of Canada, Nova Scotia and New Brunswick requesting their co-operation in encouraging the growth of that product as well as flax.[5] In 1785 orders were sent to the Governor of Quebec, which, as in the case of timber, gave the Government a pre-emption right on all lands suitable for such naval necessities. In all surveys of land, the surveyor was to report the quantity of lands fit for the production of hemp and flax. "You are to take particular care to insert a clause in every grant of land where any part thereof is fit for such production, obliging the Grantee annually to sow a proportional part of his grant with hemp and flax seed."[6] This

[1] See Franklin's *Works*, IV, p. 225, quoted by Beer, G. L., *op. cit.*, pp. 95–6.

[2] Sheffield, *Observations*, etc., p. 48.

[3] In 1764 a new bounty was granted on hemp from the British Colonies, 4 Geo. III, c. 26, and in 1767 valuable premiums were added. In 1770 a fund was established to encourage the spread of the industry. Anderson, *op. cit.*, Vol. IV, pp. 50 and 137; also see (Brit. Mus.) Add. MS. 8133 C, fol. 149.

[4] Report of Adam Lymburner, Feb. 9, 1788; C.O. 42/12, fol. 241. Both flax and hemp required a light, rich, fertile soil, but unlike most crops could be reared for a few years in succession. Generally 3 bushels were sown to the acre.

[5] B.T. 5/4, fols. 324 and 336–7.

[6] Additional Instructions to Governor of Quebec regarding the Granting of Lands; B.T. 6/102.

policy received additional support in the following year, when two bills were passed providing bounties on the importation of hemp and undressed flax from British America.[1]

But the industry required more than ordinary aids to overcome the handicaps which beset a country in the pioneering stage. The acquisition of thousands of loyalists was already being felt, but theirs was still a fight for subsistence, and pioneers were apt to cast more consideration upon their own livelihood than upon the British Navy. Furthermore, the country was suffering from the lack of a proper code of commercial law, a legacy of the Quebec Act. George Allsopp, the stormy petrel of the Legislative Council, was right when he declared that " the laws and Customs of Canada, which form the most imperfect system in the world for a commercial people, have in matters of trade been long since exploded in France, and the Code Marchand introduced in all their towns in its stead."[2]

Shortly after his arrival in England in 1788 as agent for the English party in Canada, Adam Lymburner, a leading business man and politician of Quebec, attempted to explain the situation to the British Government. The *Parliamentary History* contains the gist of his opinions in the form of a scathing diatribe on the confusion and uncertainty prevalent under the existing régime.[3] In a private report to Pitt[4] he pointed out that " the custom of Paris intended solely for the regulation of Landed Property, Descent, etc., was digested into a system in the sixteenth century, when Trade and Commerce were in their infancy and very little attended to or respected in that Kingdom. In an infant colony such as Canada, many articles might be raised and much of the rude proceeds of the Lands so far manufactured as to produce great riches to the Province and be of great service to the Empire at large.[5] But as things

[1] *Lords' Journals*, XXXVII, 5226.

[2] On March 6, 1780, Allsopp presented a paper entitled " Reasons and Protest against the Notes, Resolution and address to the Governor of the Legislative Council." C.O. 45/3.

[3] Speech of Lymburner, May 18, 1788. See also speech of Powys in support. *Parl. History*, Vol. 27, pp. 511–2.

[4] Lymburner to William Pitt, Jan. 24, 1788 ; Chatham MS. 346.

[5] Attorney-General Monk is reported to have declared, in the manner of Lymburner, that " the ideas of the Canadians are very circumscribed, no kind of government but one upon the most liberal principles of freedom will enable

must come in competition at market with the same articles from other states long in the practice of raising and preparing them, bounties and other encouragements would be necessary for some years." The climate and soil of Canada, he added, were especially well adapted to the culture of hemp.[1]

Lymburner's advocacy of schemes of agricultural encouragement received a warmer hearing than his petitions for reform of the commercial law,[2] and merely fortified the Colonial Secretary in the policy which the Government were preparing to forward. In September of 1787, Sydney had written to Dorchester with regard to bounties which might be offered in Canada for the cultivation of hemp.[3] This time he requested his advice on exportation facilities and on the pecuniary inducements which might be held out. He also asked for an estimate on the price of import to England, so that a comparison might be made between the supplies which might be drawn from Canada, and those which were at present received from foreign countries.

Dorchester referred the questionnaire to an active and diligent organization known as the Agricultural Society. In the meantime, he reported to Sydney his own faith in the future of the three provinces as producers of hemp and flax, provided that premiums and bounties were sufficiently attractive.[4] A

this country to be a commercial one. A good government cannot remedy the inconvenience of climate, which is an incurable evil, but the country is capable of great improvements and has resources in itself superior to most of the northern parts of the Continent of America, if properly attended to and encouraged." Letter from Manchut, June 6, 1786. (Brit. Mus.) Add. MS. 38346, fols. 359-60.

[1] For evidence of Lymburner's statement, see "Observations of Mr. Collins on the Cultivation of Hemp and Flax at the New Settlements," in Appendix to Report of Committee of Council for Commerce and Police, March 3, 1787; C.O. 45/7.

[2] In view of the complicated nature of the problem it was considered unwise to alter the commercial laws before the proposed Canada Act of 1791 was drawn up. As in the case of the Quebec Revenue Act, so with the commercial code, the Bill provided for no alterations. The Secretary of State, Grenville, wrote to Dorchester in June of 1790, that "After much enquiry and consideration, and after receiving the opinions of professional men upon the subject, it does not appear to me to be practicable to introduce into the proposed bill any considerable or material articles of Commercial Law, and the insertion of those of smaller importance would not be desirable." Grenville to Dorchester, Whitehall, June 5, 1790. Shortt and Doughty, *op. cit.*, Vol. II, p. 1024.

[3] Sydney to Dorchester, Sept. 14, 1787; C.O. 42/51, fol. 93.

[4] Dorchester to Sydney, Quebec, July 10, 1788, No. 75; C.O. 42/59.

second letter to Nepean was similarly optimistic in tone and included a request for 200 bushels of seed for distribution.[1]

According to the Agricultural Society, no hemp had been cultivated in the province since the conquest, and it was difficult to procure accurate information.[2] They agreed, however, that the climate and soil of many parts of the province were well adapted to its culture. "We are strongly of the opinion," the recommendation concluded, "that if the culture of hemp could be rendered general in this province, though every farmer cultivated but a small part of his farm with that article, the quantity produced in the whole province would be very considerable at the same time that it would interfere very little with the other branches of husbandry, a great part of the labour being performed at a season of inactivity. The resources of the country for the payment of the British manufactures imported into it might be doubled and that by furnishing a raw material of most essential utility to the Navy and Commerce of the Mother Country, which we are of opinion would, by the encouragement we have proposed, become generally cultivated in this province, before the expiration of seven years." They expressed the belief that if the Government offered to purchase all the hemp that might be raised in the province for seven years at fixed rates, many of the farmers could be induced to apply part of their ground and labour to the production of possibly several thousand tons. They provided estimates of prices which might be offered, based on allowance for bounty and freight, and taking into consideration the average price of Russian hemp since 1783.[3] They further urged the free distribution of from 2,000 to 4,000 bushels of seed, and the granting of premiums for the greatest quantity raised in each parish.[4] The expense of both seed and premiums, they

1 Dorchester to Nepean, Quebec, Nov. 4, 1788; C.O. 42/63. Nepean referred the letter to Cottrell, Jan. 14, 1789; C.O. 42/12, fol. 245.

2 Legislative Council Report, Feb. 2, 1790; C.O. 45/11, fol. 5.

3 The Society's suggested ratings were as follows:—

Hemp of the first quality, equal to "Russian clean"	£35 per ton (current).
Hemp of the second quality, equal to "outshot"	£33 per ton.
Hemp of the third quality, equal to "half clean" ...	£31 10*s*. per ton.
Hemp of the fourth quality, equal to Codille ...	£23 per ton.

4 £5 current was offered for the greatest quantity raised fit for sale, not inferior in quality to that known as Russian "half clean," nor less in quantity than one ton. £2 10*s*. for the next greatest quantity of same quality and not less than ½-ton; C.O. 45/11, fol. 5.

claimed, should not exceed £1,500 sterling and such an encouragement need only be required for the first year. But an even more important concern was the fear that lack of skill might endanger the beginnings of the industry.[1] In order to avoid the hazards of doubtful experiment they urged that a few people from European countries, thoroughly experienced in raising hemp and skilled in dressing it, should be engaged to settle in Canada and act as instructors.[2]

The Committee of the Quebec Legislative Council accepted the Agricultural Society's programme and referred it to Dorchester on March 2. The Governor, on his own initiative, immediately ordered that all hemp, the growth of the province, offered for sale at Quebec and Montreal, should be purchased on the account of the Government at the following prices:

Russian Quality . .	£35
Second Quality . .	£33
Third Quality . .	£31
Fourth Quality . .	£23

These prices were to hold good until July 1, 1798.[3]

In a letter to Grenville, the new Colonial Secretary, he explained the rather high premiums as necessary to counter the higher market prices in the United States.[4] He asked that quantities of seed be sent out for distribution, that a dozen sets of Russian hemp of the four different qualities be sent out as standards for the surveys, and finally that a few experienced families from Russia or Germany be procured to assist in establishing the industry.

The Board of Trade held a long discussion on the substance of Dorchester's letter.[5] They called in the Comptroller of the Navy and various Naval Commissioners who delivered long

[1] Agricultural Society Minutes; C.O. 42/67.

[2] The cultivation of hemp and flax was a highly skilled operation. The crop had to be pulled before the capsules were quite ripe (" when they are just beginning to change from a green to a pale brown colour and when the stalks of the plant have become yellow throughout about two-thirds of their height "). The operation to prepare it for market involved pulling, rippling, retting, drying, rolling and scutching. For hemp the method of gathering and retting was similar to flax, but as a rule it was a harder plant than flax, was much coarser and more brittle, and did not require the same amount of attention during the first few weeks of its growth.

[3] C.O. 45/11, fol. 42.

[4] Dorchester to Grenville, Quebec, March 6, 1790; C.O. 42/67 (No. 17).

[5] Aug. 24, 1790; B.T. 5/6.

and melancholy papers, heavily freighted with statistics on the situation at home and the prospects in Canada. The Comptroller, Charles Middleton, went to the root of the situation in a few grave words. "It is of the utmost consequence to His Majesty's service that the hemp made use of in the Navy should be of the first quality, as the safety of our ships must depend on the goodness of our cables and cordage."[1]

The average consumption of hemp in the Navy during the war had been about 10,000 tons; in peace from 2,500 to 3,000; of this amount one-third was the imported Riga variety and two-thirds St. Petersburg. Furthermore, the price of the commodity had continued to rise since 1756.[2] On the other hand, there was very little difference between St. Petersburg prices and those held out by the Governor and Council in Canada. Moreover to the Canadian rate would be added freight of £3 a ton, with the risks of damage and the loss to the revenue through the absence of a duty. Canadian hemp would probably cost £40 a ton, and even then only a small part might prove fit for naval purposes. It had been proved, according to the Comptroller, that American hemp hitherto imported had sustained a loss of one half the weight in the course of manufacture.

The Minutes of the Committee of the Privy Council for Trade reflect in turn the discouragement which the reports of the Naval Commissioners occasioned. Comparison with the production of foreign countries did little to disperse gloom, but stiffened determination. France raised much of her own hemp, and French cordage was fully as good as, if not better than, English. Dutch cordage surpassed the home product and the Spanish variety was much superior. Evidence seemed to indicate that Canada might become, with industry and proper aids, a hemp-producing country. Dependence on foreign stores must be relieved at any cost, and Canada appeared

[1] B.T. 5/6, fol. 299 (Paper No. 1). See also C.O. 42/12, fol. 648, and Minutes of the Committee of the Privy Council for Trade, Sept. 8, 1790; C.O. 43/10.

[2] The average price of Riga hemp in the French war (1752-62) was £30 13*s.* 2*d.* of Petersburg clean £26 11*s.* 5*d.* During peace (1767–74) Riga was £31 12*s.* o*d.* and Petersburg £26 15*s.* 5*d.*, so that peace prices exceeded war prices. From 1775 to 1782, Riga cost £37 15*s.* o*d.* and Petersburg £33 2*s.* 6*d.* Following the American Revolution there was a lowering to £33 2*s.* o*d.* and £28 6*s.* o*d.* (which included a duty of £3 13*s.* 4*d.* and freight insurance); B.T. 5/6, fol. 299.

the most likely source of salvation. " It is of so much importance to this country as a Maritime State," resolved the Committee, " to obtain if possible a supply from some part of His Majesty's Dominions, and not to depend on Foreign Dominions, that His Majesty's Government should continue to encourage in every proper way and at any reasonable charge every attempt which the zeal of His Majesty's subjects may induce them to make for the production of so useful a commodity."[1]

The Committee therefore felt obliged to concur with Dorchester's recommendations. Two thousand bushels of seed and the sample set of Russian hemp should be sent out as the Governor had proposed. They approved of the offering of premiums, but were inclined to deprecate his engagement of the previous March, whereby the Government undertook to buy all the hemp at a fixed price until July 1, 1798. This regulation they admitted would induce growth, but was most liable to abuse, as tending to produce inferior grades. Vital necessity rendered financial considerations of lesser consequence. Nevertheless, there remained one difficulty. Although the high prices offered must be met, the money could not come out of the public revenue without the consent of Parliament.[2]

The Government had come to grips with a difficult task and they pursued their programme in Canada with the same tenacity they had displayed in forcing hemp culture in England. Russian samples and seed were sent in quantity.[3] There was some difficulty in securing experienced instructors,[4] but a few skilled persons were finally engaged to initiate the widespread cultivation.[5] The additional aid of handsome bounties was expected to produce results. On the whole the response was feeble. Governors' instructions in the 'nineties continued to

[1] Minutes of Committee of Privy Council for Trade, Sept. 8, 1790; B.T. 5/6, fol. 324, and C.O. 43/10.

[2] *Ibid.*

[3] See Watson to Bernard, London, Jan. 17, 1791; C.O. 42/85.

[4] Secretary François Motz (to Nepean ?, in French) referred to the obstacles in the way of engaging men to teach the process of hemp culture. " The first public notice to engage families would, in Prussia, involve perpetual imprisonment, and in Russia, slavery in Siberia; then there was the repugnance of German families to the sea voyage." As it happened the Committee were not in favour of sending German families, for in their opinion the best hemp was grown in Poland and Livonia; B.T. 5/6, fol. 324.

[5] Grenville to Dorchester, Whitehall, March 7, 1791; C.O. 42/73, fol. 132.

urge the demands of the Admiralty for good hemp and flax, but dependence on continental sources remained ever a forbidding spectre. Cultivation was carried on fairly extensively, but management and preparation were bad. Only after some years did Upper Canada produce sufficient hemp for her own supply of cordage. In Lower Canada, the experiments had entirely failed.[1]

To what extent during the eighteenth century England's relations with Russia were influenced by this desperate need for flax, hemp and lumber is a matter of diplomatic history.[2] To the England of that day, the problem of naval supply continued to provoke anxiety and effort until steel hulls replaced the rotting wood, and steel wire hawsers the hempen fibres of Russia and the Colonies.[3]

[1] Anderson, David, *Canada—or a view of the importance of the British American Colonies*, p. 231. In 1814 appeals were still urgent. There were 300,000, out of a population of 360,000, engaged in agriculture. If every Canadian farmer grew one acre of hemp, it was urged, the British supply would be complete.

[2] The problem of naval supply still figured in British diplomacy with Russia, at least to 1812. Sir Thomas Byam Martin wrote to Sir Henry Martin on May 26 of that year urging the subsidizing of Sweden. "The Swedes are in close alliance with Russia, and it is thought the completion of the present negotiation would prove an immediate stepstone to our reconciliation with Russia, which would in very great degree repay the subsidy by giving us naval stores at half the present cost . . . to say nothing of the good timber we should get, in any quantity, instead of the rotten stuff from America." *Letters and Papers of Sir Thomas Byam Martin*, II, p. 176.

[3] Not until after 1811 were hempen cables substituted in part by iron and then by steel wire hawsers. A first-rate ship generally carried eleven hemp cables, the largest being 25-in. (equal to a 2¼-in. iron cable), 600-ft. in length and weighing 6 tons.

For the story of the transformation from wooden to iron ships in the Merchant and Royal Navy in the 1850's, see "The Last Years of the Navigation Acts," Clapham, J. H., *E.H.R.*, Vol. XXV (1910), pp. 687–707.

CHAPTER VIII

THE VESTIBULE OF COMMERCE

THE boundary of 1783 which followed the natural line of lake and river westward into the unknown had severed many geographic unities. The Great Lakes system had provided an easy mode of division in the eyes of statesmen who had studied doubtful eighteenth-century maps, and whose carelessness had led to the assumption that the Mississippi was linked by the Red River to Lake Winnipeg.

The concern of the British treaty makers had been trade, not territory, and trade depended on easy communications. In retaining the St. Lawrence River, along with privileges of free trade on the Mississippi, they had secured two mighty water routes whose long continued importance had provoked rivalry and bloodshed between Frenchmen and Englishmen ever since the days of La Salle.[1] The history of British American relationships, even after the American Revolution, continued to be affected, if not dominated, by the significance of these highways of trade.

In the North America of one hundred and fifty years ago, water transport played an immensely greater part in the domestic economy of the country than it does to-day. The coastal states were separated from each other by barriers of mountain, desert or swamp, while the interior was cut off from the coast by the massive Appalachian range. Almost the only means of carriage between the back country and the sea was provided by the little schooners, sloops and jebecco boats which found ready access through the St. Lawrence during five short months of navigation, or ascended the broad reaches of the Mississippi. Actually it was easier for farmers in Western Pennsylvania on the Upper Ohio to send their heaviest produce

[1] An excellent article by W. T. Morgan, in the *Canadian Historical Review*, March, 1929, discusses this early rivalry under the title of "English Fear of Encirclement in the Seventeenth Century."

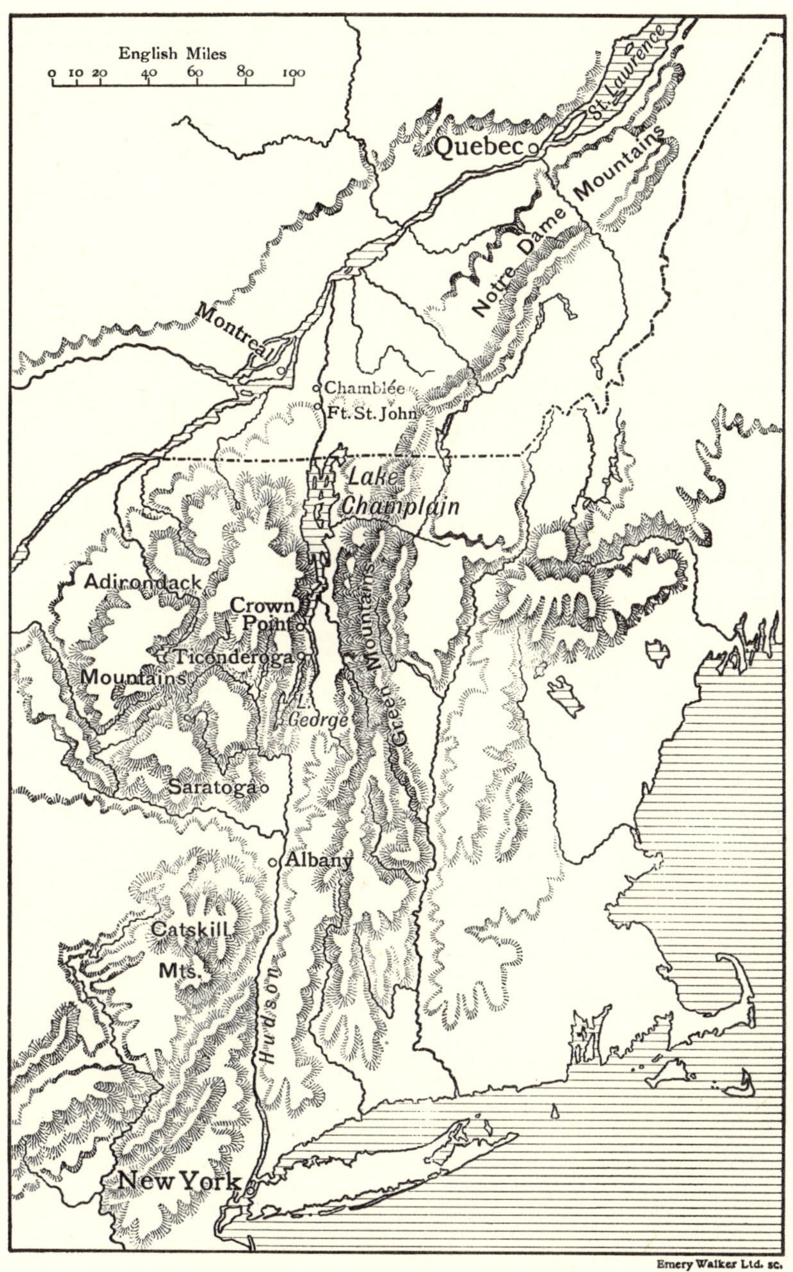

VERMONT AND THE LAKE CHAMPLAIN ROUTE.

to Philadelphia by way of New Orleans than directly overland.[1]

Because their prosperity depended on sure communication by water, Vermont, Kentucky and Tennessee delayed joining the Confederation beyond the mountains. The fact that Kentucky and Tennessee were altogether dependent on the Mississippi River, which Spain held closed at the delta, almost entirely gave rise to the labyrinth of intrigues between those states and Spain, France and England in respect to Mississippi privileges. In the case of Vermont, there developed a connection with Britain which might at one time have grown into a political as well as an economic union. Three years in particular, 1789 to 1792, provide fascinating studies in back-door diplomacy during a period when foreign powers competed in their efforts to loosen the allegiance of Western settlements to the Congress of Confederation.[2] But all inducements were in vain, Kentucky, Tennessee, Vermont, one by one succumbed to the conciliatory efforts of the new United States. In the case of Vermont a highly complicated diplomacy had in final reckoning achieved nothing. Yet, for ten years and more, the economic life of that state was regulated by the British Navigation system.

Hemmed within its own uncertain boundaries by the Green Mountains and the northern links of the Appalachian Chain, obstacles far more formidable than the Rockies of to-day, Vermont found ready access to the sea only by way of Lake Champlain and the Richelieu. The tempting pathway which Burgoyne had followed to disaster in 1777 now provided a simple water route between the towering Adirondacks and Green Mountains to the St. Lawrence, above Montreal.

From the beginning the British Government had appreciated this natural dependence. Germaine had written to Haldimand shortly before his fall instructing him to use all his power to secure Vermont, and through her leaders to diffuse the King's

[1] Bemis, S. F., *Jay's Treaty*, pp. 17–18, *passim*; *History of Domestic and Foreign Commerce of the U.S.*, by Johnson, E. R. and others (Carnegie Institute, 1915), p. 205.

[2] See Turner, F. J., "Correspondence of the French Ministers to the United States, 1791–7," in American Historical Association *Annual Reports*, 1903; "English Policy towards America, 1790–1," in *A.H.R.*, Vols. VII and VIII; and "Policy of France toward the Mississippi Valley," *ibid.*, X.

good intentions. Haldimand was willing but doubtful. "No pains on my part shall be wanting," he declared, "towards effecting His Majesty's wishes in reclaiming the inhabitants of Vermont, although I fear there is little hope of success. They are in general a profligate Banditti totally without principle and now become desperate."[1]

The Governor was over-cautious and a trifle prejudiced. The advantages in trade to be derived from a British connection appealed to a good many individuals in Vermont. They presented a sound argument against joining the new union with its heavy load of debt and other implied responsibilities. Many men favoured an alliance or even political union with Great Britain. The leaders of this separatist party were the Allen brothers, Ethan, Ira and Levi, the former of whom had won laurels in the victory at Ticonderoga in 1776. Their attitude and that of their confrères was quite clearly enunciated by Governor Thomas Chittenden on July 25, 1780, in a letter to the President of Congress. Chittenden denied the right of Congress to determine the claims of jurisdiction set up by the inhabitants of Vermont, ". . . for on proviso that neither Congress nor the legislatures of those states which they represent will support Vermont in their independence, but devote her to the usurped Government of any other power, she has not the most distant motive to continue hostilities with Great Britain and maintain an important frontier for the benefit of the United States, and for no other reward than the ungrateful one of being enslaved by them."

The humiliating surrender of Cornwallis for a time put a damper on the aspirations of the party, although Ira Allen was still of the opinion that there was a very considerable number "who dreaded the arbitrary measures of Congress." That body in their hour of triumph had threatened to divide the province among three claimant states unless she came to terms and this form of intimidation revived the flame of opposition.[2] In April of 1783 Allen wrote to Haldimand that "the legislature here is determined to be annexed to Canada and to become a royal government."[3]

[1] Haldimand to Secretary of State in Sept. 13, 1779; C.O. 42/14, fol. 188.

[2] Letter of Ira Allen, No. 4, 1781. (Brit. Mus.) Add. MS. 21835, fol. 162. C.A. (1888), p. 787.

[3] Arlington, April 10, 1783. *Ibid.*, fol. 188 and C.A. (1888), p. 789.

His surmise seemed likely to be justified. Not long after the peace had been signed, commissioners from Governor Chittenden began paying periodic visits to Haldimand to treat for a free trade.[1] They asserted that the state was strongly opposed to joining confederation, even though Congress should relieve them of a share of the joint debt. They as much as told the Governor that Vermont must either become annexed to Canada or become mistress of it as it was the only channel by which their produce could be marketed.[2]

On September 10, Ira Allen wrote in similar strain.[3] The people of Vermont were waiting for free trade. They considered themselves " unconnected with any power and by natural situation were inclined to Canada for commerce." With a restraint uncommon among colonial governors, Haldimand replied that he could not open free trade with Vermont before he received instructions and knew the measures adopted by the British Government. Being desirous, however, of " harmony and good neighbourhood," he would permit Vermont to send in cattle and grain and to receive clothing.[4] Nevertheless, the Governor took pains to add that such temporary importations should be subject to proper restrictions and permissible only with the understanding that Governor Chittenden should take steps to prevent illicit trade. But with the exception of spasmodic contributions of food, this limited permission led to no regular commerce. Haldimand the soldier had a scrupulous respect for legality, and to him the Trade and Navigation Laws bore the sanctity of the Ten Commandments. " We have no communications with the neighbouring states," said Councillor Findlay. " If the Governor would permit the Vermonters to come in and purchase British manufactures, the stores in Montreal and Quebec would soon be emptied, but he is against it. The merchants

[1] See Council Minutes, March 4, 1784; C.O. 45/4.

[2] Haldimand to North, Quebec, October 24, 1783; Shortt and Doughty, *op. cit.*, II, p. 735; Haldimand Collection (Brit. Mus.) Add. MS. 21835. Quoted by Bemis in " Relations between Vermont Separatists and Great Britain," *A.H.R.* (1915–6), p. 21.

[3] Ira Allen to Haldimand, Montreal, Sept. 10, 1784; Haldimand Collection (Brit. Mus.) Add. MS. 21835, fol. 244 and C.A. (1888), p. 794.

[4] Haldimand to Ira Allen, Sept. 17, 1784 (Brit. Mus.), Add. MS. 21835, fol. 246.

grumble confoundedly and cannot conceive his reasons for refusing to accept of American gold for English goods."[1]

On receipt of the Allen correspondence Sydney was inclined to adopt for the time being an attitude of *laisser-faire.* It would not be consistent with the Treaty of 1783 to interfere openly in the disputes of Vermont and the United States, although it would be difficult to refuse to take them under protection should they determine to become subjects of Great Britain.[2] In the meantime the subject of trade relations might be considered apart. Sydney, therefore, referred the whole matter to the Board of Trade who based their report largely on the evidence of Carleton and Haldimand. One notes again the continued and profound respect of the Colonial Office for Carleton's views on Canadian affairs, and the almost literal acceptance of his verdicts as infallible. On this occasion Carleton repeated in part the arguments which bolstered Sheffield's case in 1784.[3] He reiterated the astonishing statement that he did not foresee any instance in which the Province of Quebec could want any assistance either in Lumber or Provisions from the countries belonging to the United States. The produce of Canada was the same as that of all the Northern Countries belonging to the States. Rice which could not be grown in Canada might be brought from the Southern Provinces, but if admitted it would tend to diminish the consumption of their own grain and consequently check agriculture. Some bad tobacco was grown, but it answered the purpose. With regard to the possibilities of direct communication by land and inland navigation, he refused to give a decided opinion. Conditions might conceivably alter with the times, and perhaps certain powers should be left with the governor to act according to circumstances.

Haldimand, who had lowered the trade bars sufficiently to save Canada from hunger in 1783, echoed Carleton's sentiments.[4] Cultivation was likely to improve greatly; there was no need for American provisions, and imports would discourage cultivation. He referred to his own severity in pro-

[1] Findlay to Skene, Montreal, March 6, 1784; C.O. 42/16.

[2] Sydney to Haldimand, April 8, 1784; see Bemis, *A.H.R.*, p. 548 also contained in Canadian Archives, Q., 23/55.

[3] Council Chamber, Whitehall, March 7 to 14, 1785; B.T. 5/2, fol. 220.

[4] *Ibid.*

hibiting intercourse by land, particularly in the matter of peltry and French products. He had from time to time allowed cattle and timber to be brought into the provinces, and had encouraged the sale of British manufactures to the Americans—though never without a permit.

The Committee adopted the views of its witnesses in two resolutions.[1] There must be no importation of American goods by sea.[2] In the matter of intercourse by land and inland navigation, the Governor was to instruct the Legislative Council of Quebec to prepare an ordinance for preventing the carrying of any peltry out of the province into the United States, and also to enforce laws for preventing the bringing of any foreign rum or spirits or any goods or manufacture of any foreign European countries or of Asia from the United States into Quebec.

With the exception of two sharp thorns, St. Pierre and Miquelon, the problem of smuggling had largely disappeared when Canada fell to Britain in 1763. On the withdrawal of the southern colonies as a separate nation it had a natural tendency to revive, encouraged by the fact that the Americans were often ready to pay a higher price for peltry.[3] Tea remained the most important article of inland contraband, and by sea the principal object was wine.[4] It has been noted in a previous chapter that the profit on rum was not yet sufficient to induce an illicit trade of any magnitude.[5]

Haldimand had always made every effort to discourage the practice. In 1784 he made a fervently patriotic speech before the Legislative Council, in which he declared, " I shall continue to exert my utmost efforts to protect the commerce of the Province and to render it useful to the Mother Country by preventing, as much as in me lies, the fur trade from being diverted by interested people to the neighbouring states of

[1] Court of St. James, May 4, 1785 ; C.O. 5/32 ; also contained in additional instructions to Haldimand, May 26, 1785, Shortt and Doughty, *op. cit.*, II, p. 733.

[2] On April 8, 1785, an Order in Council directed that " no Goods, the Growth or Manufacture of the Countries belonging to the United States of America should be imported into our Province of Quebec by sea." *Ibid.*, II, p. 733.

[3] B.T. 5/2, fol. 221.

[4] Dorchester to Hawkesbury, Quebec, May 17, 1788 ; C.O. 42/12, fol. 295.

[5] See Chapter VI.

America."[1] Lieutenant-Governor Hamilton followed this pronouncement by a Proclamation on March 9, 1785, prohibiting by penalties the illicit trade by way of Lake Champlain, and ordering that the laws regulating Plantation trade should be put in full force.

This rigid attitude on the part of the Home Government largely accounted for the failure of Ira Allen's subsequent negotiations. Shortly after the publication of Hamilton's manifesto he presented for the approval of the Quebec Council an Act which had been passed by the State of Vermont for the purpose of opening a free trade " to and through the Province of Quebec."[2] The Committee of Council replied that they had no authority to open up a trade with the state of Vermont, because in the words of the Lieutenant-Governor, " no commercial agreement can be entered upon by any of the Governors of His Majesty's Provinces without the sanction of the British legislature."[3] However, they gave Allen the indefinite promise that they would lay his request before the Secretary of State and communicate to him the answer.[4] As a result there was little mention of the Vermont Separatists until the autumn. Yet their work had stimulated considerable interest among certain commercial classes both in London and in Canada.

In October Silas Deane wrote to Dorchester on the subject of improving the Champlain route to the St. Lawrence by means of a canal.[5] The favourable reception of the letter adds to its interest and authority. Deane predicted a split in the confederacy between north and south. Assuming a separation he referred to the northern dependence of Maine and New York on British transportation facilities. " Their commerce should be an important object to this country, it would create a large and annually increasing demand for coarse and heavy manufactures, in return for which there would be sent into the River St. Lawrence the finest masts and spars of any in America, and in the greatest quantity for the British Navy, and beyond comparison the best oak timber of any in America for Butt,

[1] March 25, 1784; C.O. 45/4.
[2] Council Minutes, March 9, 1785; C.O. 45/4.
[3] The Commission of Governor Chittenden presented their petition on March 24, 1784. See Council Minutes, March 28, 1785; C.O. 45/4.
[4] Speech of April 14, 1785, *ibid.*
[5] Deane to Dorchester, Oct. 25, 1785; C.O. 42/66.

Pipe, Hogshead or Barrel Staves for the British and West Indian markets."

In emphasizing the advantages of his canal scheme, Deane pointed out the total insufficiency of Canada to supply lumber and masts for the Navy, all of which indicated the vital need for a Vermont and northern New England trade. " Canada had little or no pine fit for masts and no oak of any value. These deficiencies might be abundantly supplied by cutting a navigable canal from Lake Champlain around the rapids and falls of St. John's into the navigable waters below, and then opening a free trade with Vermont and with the frontiers of New England and New York. By so doing, all the trade of that extensive country (whose inhabitants had increased so rapidly) would centre in Canada, which would be of more service and benefit to Great Britain than if all that country around the Lake had been included in her American Dominions at the Peace."

Early in the following year, the London merchants made Deane's suggestion the substance of a petition and report.[1] Again it was urged that Vermont's lack of seaports was Canada's opportunity. Free access by the St. Lawrence and Champlain route would open the way to British manufactures, would be productive of great trade and riches to the Province and at the same time would secure an increase of British navigation and shipping.

Following up the attack, Levi Allen re-undertook the case for his own state. A memorial which was presented to Dorchester in March asked for absolute free commercial intercourse with Canada, along with a similar freedom of trade to the British West Indies and to England as in British vessels. Importation free of all duty and customs was requested for all sorts of lumber and ship's timber, naval stores, provisions, pot and pearl ashes or " anything else not enumerated, being the growth and produce of Vermont."[2] Peltries were excepted.

[1] London, Feb., 1786; C.O. 42/49.

That same year a bill had been passed " for the further increase and encouragement of shipping and navigation." This was to make more definite the British registry of vessels so as " to make more exclusive the navigation acts which confine trade to ships of Britain and Ireland, Guernsey, Jersey and Isle of Man or some Colonies, Plantations and Territories in Asia, Africa or America." B.T. 6/96.

[2] Allen to Dorchester, Que., Nov. 22, 1786; see C.O. 42/12; C.O. 42/51; C.O. 45/7, fol. 150. The enumerated articles included masts, spars, bowsprits,

This time the efforts of the Allen brothers and the merchants, together with a certain element of diplomatic expediency, brought success. As in the case of the French Treaty of Commerce, trade monopoly bowed before an arrangement which was essentially profitable. Lord Sydney wrote his assent and on April 18, 1787, Dorchester issued a Proclamation permitting the opening of trade by way of Lake Champlain with the "neighbouring states" to the Province of Quebec.[1] Free importation of lumber, naval stores, hemp, flax, grain, provisions, livestock and all products grown in those states was allowed, and all British products excepting furs and peltries might be exported there from Canada on payment of duty.

In April this was followed by the first ordinance of the Legislative Council regulating inland trade. As supplementary to the comprehensive proclamation, it provided for the importation of tobacco and pot and pearl ashes into the province by the inland communication of Lake Champlain and the River Sorel, and permitted their re-exportation to Great Britain.[2]

During the past few years, Canadian potash had developed into an important article of trade. The bleaching industries particularly required this article, in which Canadian maples, beeches and birch were especially rich. The first Englishman had set up the business in 1767 and three years later fifty tons had been exported.[3] Now the new ordinance offered American competition to an industry only recently established and one which Loyalists were adopting with considerable advantage. It was not unnatural therefore that the new settlers should severely criticize a measure which might interrupt a trade in the natural by-product of their forest clearing operations.[4] They made their petition an appeal for double advantage—the adoption of a regular bounty system, and a ban on the

yards, oak ship plank, pine deck plank: futlocks, knees, ship timber and lumber of every sort, kind and quality; tar, pitch, turpentine, tallow and all sorts of naval stores, iron, flax seed, hemp, honey, beef, pork, wheat, barley, peas, Indian corn, rye, butter, cheese, and all kinds of provisions; pot and pearl ashes, apples, cyder and vinegar.

[1] See C.O. 45/7, fol. 148.

A brief summary of the negotiation for free trade between Vermont and Quebec, 1786–8, is contained in the Chatham MS. 343.

[2] Passed as an Ordinance, April 27, 1787; C.O. 45/7, fol. 133.

[3] *Canada and its Provinces*, Vol. IV, Adam Shortt, Chapter on "General Economic History, 1763–1841," p. 528.

[4] Dorchester to Sydney (enclosing petition), No. 18 June 13, 1787; C.O., 42/50.

importation of Vermont pot and pearl ash, as leading incidentally to illicit trade in other articles.

The petitioners failed to enlist the sympathies of the Home Office, but the principle of the local government's right to legislate on matters of internal commerce was fought out in the Legislative Council. On July 13, 1787, a Privy Council decision had handed it down that the Governor and Council might make regulations respecting intercourse by land or inland navigation between Canada and the United States.[1] In spite of that decree it was contended that such a power militated against Home Orders-in-Council for regulating trade by sea only, between the colonies and America[2] and in particular against the Enabling Act of the 4th of April previous. By a narrow majority the disputants won their point[3] and the contest was carried overseas. In the words of the Secretary of Council—" By negativing such resolutions, the majority of the Council seemed to doubt the validity of any of the existing laws of the Province on the ground of a want of legal competency of authority in the Provincial Legislature."[4]

Private monopolies which ran counter to the general good, particularly when that good was more and more interpreted in terms of industrial expansion, were growing less in favour every day. Furthermore, the shaky condition of American constitutional existence during this period rendered it expedient that Britain should keep some slight diplomatic lever within reach. So it was not altogether strange that the Lords Committee of the Privy Council decided that Lord Dorchester had properly interpreted the Government's instructions and that " no restriction was intended to be laid on American importations by Land or Inland navigation of any commodities not prohibited by law. But, if any of the afore-mentioned commodities should be afterwards imported into Great Britain and doubts arise as to the legality, the opinion of the law officers should again be ascertained."[5]

[1] Stephen Cottrell to W. W. Grenville, Office of the Committee of Privy Council for Trade, Whitehall, April 17, 1790; Chatham MS. 343.

[2] Letter of Mr. Rose, Whitehall, Aug. 21, 1787; B.T. 5/4, and Council Minutes; C.O. 45/7, fol. 145. (Enclosed, Board of Trade Minutes, July 13, 1787).

[3] *Ibid.*; C.O. 45/7, fol. 150. A resolution in favour of the Privy Council decision of July 13 was carried in the negative, 9–7.

[4] Council Minutes; C.O. 45/7, fol. 156.

[5] Whitehall, Aug. 21, 1787; B.T. 5/4.

By this time Sydney had had ample opportunity to investigate all the varied evidence connected with the problem of a purely commercial treaty, a subject which Allen had recently raised. The decision of the Ministry was as usual influenced by vague and delicate political balancings which are beyond the scope of this study. " Considering the present situation of the State of Vermont the Secretary judged that the forming of any distinct and separate Treaty with it, at this moment must be entirely out of the question."[1] He appreciated the value of the Champlain route and appears to have favourably considered Silas Deane's proposals for improving its navigation, but with regard to a constructive policy bearing on the suggestions he was silent. There was merely a reiteration of the wearisome advice, that the Home Government would view with pain any influx of European manufactures and foreign spirits, or any export of peltry into Vermont by way of the inland channel.[2]

In the meantime Levi Allen had returned to Quebec on his perennial quest for complete freedom of trade. In July he had written to Dorchester offering to supply masts, yards and bowsprits for the Navy at specified prices.[3] The offer was forwarded to Whitehall and considered by the Admiralty Board in November. Again the response was diplomatically curt. Arrangements for supply, he was told, had been made in other quarters.[4] The reason for this flat negative is hard to understand. There may have been danger, as in the case of the larger issue of a commercial treaty, that personal negotiations with the Separatist leader might involve embarrassing entanglements with the Congressional government. In addition, there was possible ground for doubting the ability of Allen to fulfil so magnanimous an engagement.

The Allen brothers' persistency was by no means the least enviable family characteristic. In the following summer, Ethan presented yet another petition with the customary

[1] Sydney to Dorchester, Sept. 14, 1787; C.O. 42/51.
[2] *Ibid.*
[3] Received at Quebec, July 2, 1787; C.O. 42/51.
Also Dorchester to Hawkesbury, Que., Aug. 18, 1787; C.O. 42/12. Quoting Royal Navy prices for 1770, Allen remarks: " I will furnish any quantity that may be wanted at 20 per cent less than above rates, and am confident some larger may be found."
[4] Whitehall, Nov. 8, 1787; C.O. 42/51.

plea for trading concessions and the ready assertion of the willingness of Vermont to come under British rule.[1] He re-emphasized the reciprocal interest of Great Britain and Vermont, the jealousy of the United States and the threat to subjugate Vermont by reason of their natural inclination to the British interest. " The objection of Vermont to join the United States is increased by the feeling that it would expose them to the displeasure of Great Britain, ruin their commerce and involve them in debt." " Vermont," he declared, " had 15,000 troops ready to take the field." She was a small state " at first sight," but had a heavy influence in American politics, and might conceivably turn the scale, so she was well worth the attention of Great Britain. On receiving a copy of the letter, Sydney acted on his usual policy of cautious procrastination. There was no reply. Levi Allen, impatient of delay, set sail for England. There, he trusted, proximity might lend power to the memorials with which he planned to assault the Home Secretary.

In the meantime, intercourse by way of the Lake Champlain route slowly increased. Success justified further relaxation by legislation, and a bill of April 14, 1788, was passed " to further regulate the inland commerce of this Province and to extend the same."[2] The Act itself was of more significance than its ordinary phraseology seemed to imply. It established once and for all the Privy Council's decision that the provincial legislature was competent on its own authority to legislate on matters of inland commerce. It was a final admission of the validity of the Ordinance and Proclamation of the previous year, and thus represented the legal investiture of the Governor and Legislative Council with the powers of commercial regulation which had previously been claimed to belong solely to the King and Council.

The provisions of the Ordinance expressed almost identically the provisional arrangements of the Proclamation of 1787. All British goods and merchandize such as could be exported by sea were permitted to be exported by land and inland navigation. Freedom of importation by Lake Champlain and the River Sorel route was provided for certain enumerated

[1] Ethan Allen to Dorchester, Quebec, July 16, 1788 ; C.O. 42/59, fol. 497.
[2] Council Minutes, March 28, 1788 ; C.O. 45/7, fol. 188.

articles such as masts, yards, bowsprits and various sorts of timber, provisions, live animals, tar, turpentine and all kinds of naval stores.[1] Two years later the Act was extended by an amendment which admitted free of duty, pig and bar iron.[2] It was the last contribution to Vermont reciprocity before Jay's Treaty.

Unfortunately the export of Vermont produce from Quebec did not exempt it from certain alien duties on entering England. Canada as a vestibule to Vermont trade enabled Canadian merchants to reap certain profits as middle-men. On their own initiative, the Committee of the Legislative Council had therefore recommended that an extension of free importation to alien produce would restrain such trade wholly to Britain, opening " a profitable barter and mutual field of payment."[3] In July, Dorchester pointed out the advantage to the British carrying trade if American natural produce imported by way of Quebec or Montreal were shipped to England as the produce of the province.[4] The recommendation received unusually rapid response. Mainly as a result of the Governor's new and enlightened attitude with regard to inter-provincial commerce, an Act of Parliament of the same year provided that American goods when imported through the St. Lawrence were to be received in Britain as if they were of Canadian origin.[5]

Perhaps it was only a coincidence that at that very time when alien duties were abolished on Vermont produce, Levi Allen was receiving the warmest welcome of his career and his proposals for complete free trade seemed nearer to success than ever before. In the spring of 1790 war seemed imminent between England and Spain over the Nootka Sound imbroglio.[6]

[1] The demand for pitch, tar and turpentine continued to be stressed in subsequent years. Like hemp and flax, these articles were indispensable to the Navy. Curiously enough, despite every manner of experiment, the firs and pines of Canada could not afford even a minor supply. Evan Nepean to William Fawkener, Nov. 9, 1788; C.O. 42/12, fol. 633.

[2] Council Minutes, Feb. 22, 1790; C.O. 45/11, Vol. 18. See Appendix C for a note on the iron industry in Canada.

[3] *Ibid.*

[4] Dorchester to Grenville (No. 43), Quebec, July 21, 1790; C.O. 42/68.

[5] 27 Geo. III, c. 29; MacPherson, David, *op. cit.*, IV, p. 203.

[6] See Turner, F. J., " English Policy Towards America, 1790–91," *A.H.R.*, VII and VIII; also Mills, Lennox, " The Real Significance of the Nootka Sound Incident," *Canadian Historical Review*, Vol. VI (June, 1925); and Manning, W. R., " The Nootka Sound Controversy," American Historical Association, *Annual Reports*, 1904, pp. 279–479.

In May, Grenville wrote to Dorchester that it was unlikely the North American dominions would be attacked, but the United States might be encouraged by Spain to demand the cession of the frontier posts held in contravention of the Treaty of 1783.[1] In that event, the importance of having the friendship of Vermont could not be over-estimated. The commercial privileges granted to Vermont might prove of real service in attaching the people to Britain.[2]

British statesmen faced a nice problem of diplomacy, the same problem which had influenced all trade negotiations since 1783. To what degree should Vermont be conciliated by a separate treaty, and was it politically prudent, all circumstances considered, to risk giving offence to the Congress of the United States by such a measure ?[3] If any definite line of policy may be determined from that long-drawn balancing of problems, commercial and political, it would seem to be contained in this most significant pronouncement of the Committee of the Privy Council.[4] "The Lords are of opinion that, in a commercial view, it will be for the benefit of this country to prevent Vermont and Kentucky and all the other Settlements now forming in the interior parts of the great Continent of North America from becoming dependent on the Government of the United States, or on that of any other foreign country, and to preserve them on the contrary in a state of Independence and to induce them to form Treaties of Commerce and Friendship with Great Britain."

This declaration of policy represented the gist of instructions which were forwarded to Canada. Governors should play the dual rôle of secret service agent and diplomat. Outwardly, however, until the settlement of the Nootka quarrel, the Government's policy was one of polite but watchful waiting. When Grenville was assured by his American agent Beckwith that the United States would not go to war, and when Spain finally came to terms, the Vermont negotiation as a diplomatic lever was no longer required.[5] It was no longer essential to risk the

[1] Grenville to Dorchester, May 6, 1790 ; C.O. 42/67.

[2] Same to the same (No. 23), *ibid.*

[3] Report of Committee of Privy Council for Trade, April 17, 1790 ; Chatham MS. 343.

[4] *Ibid.*

[5] See Bemis, S. F., "The relations between the Vermont Separatists and Great Britain, 1789–91," *A.H.R.*, Vol. XXI (1915–6), p. 547.

hostility of the new republic by playing with the possibility of a Vermont alliance. Again Allen had failed against a complexity of circumstances which it was not in his power to resist or even to understand. He returned to the United States and in the March of 1791, Vermont entered the Union.[1]

When Vermont joined the union, to be followed shortly after by Kentucky and Tennessee, that curious *entente* between business and diplomacy came to an end.[2] But, for the period prior to that event, it is worth while to ask, from the standpoint of the reaction on Canadian policy, whether British ministries were actuated by any clear and conscious purpose in their dealings with the recalcitrant states.

There seems to be no doubt that Pitt's Government, although they clung tenaciously to the Navigation Laws, were strongly influenced in their colonial policy by the vanguard of the Industrial Revolution. An anonymous document among Pitt's papers explains better than anything else the new official attitude adopted with regard to Canada.[3] " The Fur Trade from its nature must diminish every year, particularly so, as the country settles and the animals are extirpated. The lower parts of America and Canada formerly contained much fur, but at present very little is to be procured. One inhabitant that

[1] In a letter of Nov. 27, 1791, Levi reported failure " as the juncture of the U.S. with Vermont was completed some months before I left London." He seemed chiefly worried over his nearness to success. " Had I got up the St. Lawrence last year with goods, Vermont would not have joined the Union." " The inhabitants," he continued, " may repent at leisure, and when duties are levied, they will see as much clearer as Saint Paul did after the scales fell from his eyes." C.O.42/88, fol. 339.

[2] The entrance of these states into the Union definitely put an end to British designs of permanently attaching American settlements east of the Mississippi. On the other hand it by no means put an end to British intrigues in the American West. The notorious Blount affair of 1795 showed that British diplomacy continued to weigh the possibilities of an alliance with the men of the western waters against Spanish Louisiana, even while Jay's Treaty was before the Senate for ratification. See Bemis, *Jay's Treaty*, p. 263.

[3] Chatham MS. 344. Considerations on the Propriety of Great Britain abandoning the Indian posts and coming to a good understanding with America. (July, 1794 [?]), unsigned.

The emigration of traders, such as Peter Pond, Simon MacTavish and Alexander Henry, and the significant move of the firm of Phynn and Ellice from Albany to Montreal and London, was due, according to Professor Innis, partly to the fact that the supplies of fur in the Mississippi country were being worked out. See *Transactions of the Royal Society of Canada, Third Series*, Vol. XXII, Section II, May, 1928.

A later anticipation of this situation is contained in an anonymous

cultivates his farm is of more real service to Great Britain than twenty hunters. No new settler can become a manufacturer; they must draw all their necessaries from Great Britain. Encourage the settlers in the Indian country; their produce must either go down the Mississippi or go to Canada; they will receive all their goods from thence; from their situation they can have little or no connection with the coast provinces of America—their dependence will be chiefly on Canada. . . . The only object Great Britain can have in retaining Canada in a commercial view is, that as Canada extends all along the back of America, it will at all times secure to Great Britain a sale of her manufactures, and oblige the government of America to be moderate in their duties, otherwise the goods will be smuggled in upon them. . . . Encourage the back settlers. It is from that country that we will be supplied with hemp. The settlers there will never rival us either in shipping or in sailors, nor for ages in manufactures. We will have all their trade without any expense of maintaining them—what more could you require?"[1]

On the whole this indicates a general policy pursued with caution by the British Government. Open interference was not prudent. Nevertheless, a certain turn of affairs might lead to the highly desirable establishment of a separate government for Vermont and the Mississippi States.[2] Chameleon-like diplomacy must be prepared to change with every changing circumstance. "The great object of your Lordship's endeavour," wrote Grenville secretly to Dorchester, "should therefore be to cultivate such an intercourse with the leading men in the new Settlements as might give to this

memorandum from Quebec, of April 7, 1785: "The development of the Ohio by the Americans will mean the departure of the Indians. Their hunting ground thus exhausted, they will become planters. They must force a trade for their lumber, maize, cotton and tobacco. A predilection for British manufactures will help to invite the British merchants to form commercial agreements with these Southern Americans, while the peltry trade will be engrossed by the Canada merchants and Hudson's Bay traders"; C.O. 42/47, fol. 393.

[1] Chatham MS. 344.

[2] Adam Lymburner wrote to the Committee of the Privy Council "that the seeds of disunion appears to me as very deep-rooted in their constitution from the extent of their territory and other causes." If a split should occur "the attachment of the people bordering on the British provinces may give to Great Britain a considerable degree of Political Influence in American affairs." Memoranda cited; C.O. 42/88, fol. 155.

country a facility of acting, if at any time a proper occasion should occur and permit influence and advice."[1]

For that reason the history of the period represents a strange chronology of procrastination and sudden action. The manufacturers and their merchant connections in London and Canada wanted American markets, and it is obvious that British policy was strongly influenced by their demands. On the other hand, these had to be balanced against the expediencies of a terribly tangled diplomatic situation, especially during the years 1789 to 1793. Few episodes afford such clear instances of the intimate relationship between diplomacy and "big business." As in the case of the negotiations for the Treaty of 1783, if British statesmen followed any single conscious purpose, it was fundamentally that of winning rights for British trade, and Canada was called in to play an intermediary but none the less strategetic part. "Upper Canada," declared Governor Simcoe, "might become the vestibule of trade between the increasing population of the future Mississippi valley and England, in the same way as the Netherlands were then the vestibule of commerce between the German States and England."[2]

British statesmen had dreamed a dream, as glorious and as visionary as any which had gripped La Salle or the "Grand Monarque." In the heart of North America, a new Anglo-Saxon nation should arise, linked to its Mother Country through Canada, by the strong, far-reaching arm of British commerce. It was a dim fantasy created in the smoke of an awakening industrial England—a vain chimera which vanished before it could even be called a policy. The Vermont negotiation was a substantial but merely experimental factor in a grander project.

[1] W. W. Grenville, to Dorchester, Whitehall, Oct. 20, 1789 (No. 15, secret); C.O. 42/65. See also Dorchester to Sydney, Quebec, June 7, 1789 (secret), No. 112; C.O. 42/65; also Grenville to Dorchester, May 6, 1790; C.O. 10. The *Times* of Nov. 3, 1928, published extracts from a curious memorandum (evidently submitted to Pitt), which I found in the Public Record Office. The author advocates a scheme of linking the settlements on "the Western waters" with the Hudson's Bay. Spain had closed the Mississippi; the journey to the Atlantic was long and tedious. For the rapidly spreading American settlements of the north and north-west, "a passage by Hudson's Bay would be indispensably necessary . . . in consequence of which we may promise to ourselves a full and lasting possession of the trade." C.O. 47/112.

[2] Simcoe to Dundas, June 2, 1791, quoted by Bemis, *op. cit.*, *A.H.R.*, Vol. XXVII, p. 470 (Canadian Archives, Q. 278, pp. 228–55, *passim*).

APPENDICES

APPENDIX A

ARRIVALS IN CANADIAN PORTS[1]

	Ships.	Tons.	Cargoes.
	1774.		
Great Britain ..	55	7040	Goods, the produce of Great Britain and West Indies.
West Indies ..	25	1705	Rum, sugars, molasses, coffee, salt and wines.
American Continent	76	5427	Naval stores, rum, etc., although these cargoes are usually assorted with the produce of Europe and the West Indies.
	1775.		
Great Britain ..	64	8144	
West Indies ..	15	1214	
America ..	36	2433	
	1776.		
Great Britain ..	27	4959	
West Indies ..	6	525	
America ..	16	1874	
	1777.		
Great Britain ..	43	5922	
West Indies ..	12	1008	
America ..	14	731	
	1778.		
Great Britain ..	38	6111	
West Indies ..	18	1511	
America ..	20	1923	

[1] C.O. 45/10.

CLEARANCES FROM CANADIAN PORTS

To—	Ships.	Tons.
	1774.	
Great Britain	33	4577
South Ports of Europe, Africa and West Indies	67	7115
Continent of America	51	3306
	1775.	
Great Britain	37	5784
South Europe, etc.	26	2950
America	34	2107
	1776.	
Great Britain	18	2319
South Europe, etc.	15	1159
America	17	1168
	1777.	
Great Britain	29	2210
South Europe, etc.	18	1790
America	25	1680
	1778.	
Great Britain	21	2931
South Europe, etc.	13	2273
America	38	3678

EXPORTS—1774–1778

To—	
Great Britain ..	Furs, oil, pot and pearl ash, wheat, boards and planks, staves, oak timber, staves, ash oars, flax seed.
Europe and West Indies	Cod fish, boards and planks, hoops, staves, flour, biscuit, (small) pease, wheat.
America ..	Flour, biscuits, boards and planks, hoops, staves, bullocks, pease and wheat.

C.O. 42/10.

APPENDIX B

STATEMENT OF ACCOUNTS OF DUTIES RECEIVED AND PAID BY VIRTUE 14 GEO. III, C. 88
MAY 1, 1783—MAY 1, 1790

		West India Rum Free 28 Geo. 3, C. 39.	British Brandy at 3d. per gall.	Rum, etc., from British West India at 6d. per gall.	Rum, etc., from British Colonies at 9d. per gall.	Foreign Brandy from Gt. Britain at 1s. per gall.
1783	July 1	—	161,952	39,119	1,747	10,813
	October 10	—	377	6,324	278	8,699
1784	January 5	—	—	637	240	—
	July 5	—	23,957	—	—	—
	October 10	—	—	13,169	—	351
1785	January 5	—	2,895	—	—	—
	July 5	—	91,687	10,993	—	4,444
	October 10	—	5,243	—	591	—
1786	January 5	—	—	2,630	120	—
	July 5	—	3,913	54,755	334	1,237
	October 10	—	—	61,648	—	99
1787	January 5	—	—	21,853	—	—
	July 5 (Gaspée, 1785–6), New Carlisle, 1786	—	1,078	—	—	—
	July 5, Quebec	—	135	14,578	—	—
	October 10, D. & L. Foreign Spirits ...	—	4,461	15,375	—	—
	October 10	—	43,065	—	—	—
1788	January 5	—	26,978	—	—	—
	July 5	—	45,770	26,474	5,731	5,848
	October 10, Gaspée	—	400	1,170	—	—
	October 10, Quebec	—	8,409	82,938	2,059	—
1789	January 5, Gaspée	—	280	—	460	—
	January 5, Quebec	3,153	—	—	—	—
	July 5	10,478½	5,068	30,308½	—	22
	October 10 (Dom. & Carlisle) ...	9,978½	14,813	18,561½	—	—
1790	January 5, Quebec	8,065	—	—	—	—
	Total ...	31,675	440,481	400,533	11,560	31,513

Statement of Account of Spirits, Molasses, Wine and Salt Imported from May 1, 1783, to May 1, 1790

Year	Date	Molasses in British or Quebec ships at 3d. per gall.	Molasses in other ships at 6d. per gall.	Quarterly Receptions by Collector. £ s. d.	Duties sterling annually received also by Collector. £ s. d.	Paid by Collection British Treasury. £ s. d.
1783	July 1	52,524	24,579	4879 11 3	—	—
	October 10	4,982	30,072	1422 5 3	6668 6 0	6001 13 9
1784	January 5	27,324	—	366 9 3	—	—
	July 5	—	—	299 9 3	789 3 0	647 12 3¼
	October 10	8,534	—	453 10 0	—	—
1785	January 5	—	—	36 3 9	—	—
	July 5	25,701	—	1964 7 6	—	—
	October 10	100,325	—	1341 15 3	3953 6 9	3526 3 0
1786	January 5	46,156	—	647 4 0	—	—
	July 5	12,569	—	1649 5 6	—	—
	October 10	73,144	19,524	2948 10 0	5917 0 6	5395 5 11
1787	January 5	61,834	—	1319 5 0	—	—
	July 5, (Gaspée, 1785–6)	1,766	—	1209 10 9	—	—
	July 5, New Carlisle, 1786	510	—	—	—	—
	July 5, Quebec	64,118	—	—	3862 8 0	2841 4 3
	October 10	83,929	—	2027 11 3	—	—
	October 10, D. & L. Foreign Spirits ...	—	—	625 6 0	—	—
1788	January 5, D. & L. Foreign Spirits ...	23,046	—	2323 8 9	—	—
	July 5	46,572	—	—	—	—
	October 10, Gaspée	290	—	3440 5 9	5804 8 3	5016 18 4½
	October 10, Quebec	91,701	—	—	—	—
1789	January 5, Gaspée	540	100	40 13 9	—	—
	January 5, Quebec	795	—	—	—	—
	July 5	2,601	21,520	1391 11 6	—	—
	October 10 (Dom. and Carlisle) ...	109,973	—	2024 11 3	4591 1 6	3982 4 9
1790	January 5, Quebec	27,449	33,257	1174 10 9	—	—
	Total ...	866,383	129,052	£31585 5 9	£27411 14 0	£27411 2 4

One difference on charges of collection in seven years being £4,174 11*s*. 8*d*., equal to £596 7*s*. 4*d*. per annum, or nearly 13½ per cent on collection.

Contained in *Council Minutes*; C.O. 45/11, fol. 84.

	Foreign Brandy Gallons	Rum Puncheons.	Hogs-heads.	Brandy Pipes.	Hogs-heads.	Pipes.	Tierces.	Pipes.	Hogs-heads.	Casks.	Salt.
1783 ...	—	3,156	21	2,009	28	1,613	91	809	2,771	678	35,685
1784 ...	—	179	37	272	5	185	—	92	1,885	6	15,290
1785 ...	—	1,420	28	1,040	18	1,932	86	362	1,229	17	102,869
1786 ...	—	3,932	15	15	—	2,133	14	513	2,213	140	38,855
1787 ...	86,865	1,366	—	—	—	2,000	—	505	3,513	93	57,260
1788 ...	—	1,357	—	585	—	1,484	—	976	1,266	96	96,850
1789 ...	—	2,628	—	197	—	2,080	69	283	1,980	60	16,400
Total ...	86,865	14,038	101	4,118	51	11,427	260	3,540	14,857	1,090	363,189

1 Puncheon contains 110 gallons.
1 Hogshead ,, 63 ,,
1 Pipe ,, 115 ,,
1 Tierce ,, 40 ,,

D. & L. = Davison & Lees Foreign Spirits.

C.O. 45/11, fol. 87.

APPENDIX C

NOTE ON THE IRON INDUSTRY IN CANADA

IRON forges had been in operation in Canada since about 1736, and some quantities of the unwrought product had been sent to France. The ore used was a pure oxide of iron deposited from the waters of St. Maurice, and it appears to have been esteemed superior to Swedish or other European products in quality and toughness.[1] After the conquest, the English continued to use the forges until 1765, when Haldimand, Governor of Three Rivers, left for New York. Carleton revived the lease in 1767, and in three years' time some 400,000 pounds of bar iron were produced in addition to stoves and pots.

Despite varied attempts to undertake the exploitation of mines around Lake Superior,[2] by 1788 the ore bed at St. Maurice was the only one in productive use. It remained royal property, and during the whole period no single individual was able to obtain permission to establish a privately owned foundry.[3] Again and again Dorchester urged the adoption of a system of private enterprise, with the abolition of the harmful restrictions. " Canada," declared the governor, " abounds in this metal and hope may be entertained of her being able, with the advantage of wood and water, after a few years encouragement, to greatly lessen the dependence of Great Britain for this article upon foreign nations."[4] For the time being, however, the Government were satisfied to supplement their single resource with the Vermont product, and the local ordinance of March, 1790, provided for free importation.

[1] Journal of an Officer who travelled over a part of the West Indies and of North America, 1764–5; (Brit. Mus.) King's MS., 213.

[2] In 1768 Henry Bostich organized a company to undertake the exploitation of mines " in, about and under Lake Superior in North America and the islands therein and the countries all round the said Lake within the distance of 60 miles thereof." Board of Trade, Aug. 12, 1768; C.O. 5/25; see Gage to Hillsborough, Nov. 28, 1770: *Acts of Privy Council, Colonial*, unbound, p. 483.

[3] *Council Minutes*; C.O. 45/11, fol. 14.

[4] Dorchester to Sydney, Que., July 28, 1788; C.O. 42/61.

BIBLIOGRAPHY

ALTHOUGH general and special works have naturally been of great value, this book is based on a study of the sources. The chief of these consists of the unprinted public papers and the official correspondence of the Colonial Office and the Board of Trade deposited in the Public Record Office, London. The records of the Colonial Office include the original correspondence of the Secretary of State *to* and *from* the governors in Canada, the Sessional Papers or Minutes of the Quebec Council and the reports and correspondence of the Board of Trade.

I have been fortunate in finding transcripts of most of the Shelburne MSS. (now at Ann Arbor, Michigan) with Messrs. Stevens and Brown, 4, Trafalgar Square, W.C.2, who were most willing and generous in permitting my access to them. This source, together with Wharton's *Diplomatic Correspondence of the American Revolution*, was of particular value in dealing with important phases of the Settlement in 1783.

The Chatham Papers preserved at the Record Office—containing the correspondence and public papers of William Pitt —were particularly valuable for the study of the Vermont negotiation and the Mississippi project. Anglo-American relations during that period have been quite thoroughly dealt with by Professor F. J. Turner and Professor S. F. Bemis; but I have attempted to discuss the problem almost entirely from the point of view of Canada, in her capacity as a strategic highway or "vestibule of commerce" for the British trader. Documents which have been published in the *American Historical Review* by Professor Turner, or in collections such as the Haldimand MSS. in the British Museum have been used; but I have been able to obtain much good and apparently unpublished material in the Chatham Papers and in the Colonial Office Records, Series 42. The Additional MSS. proved to be a most fruitful source for miscellaneous papers and correspondence in relation to the trade of Canada.

Among the most valuable printed sources were: *Acts of the Privy Council, Colonial Series*, edited by Grant and Munro; the *Parliamentary History*; *Reports on the Canadian Archives*, edited by Douglas Brymner and later by Arthur G. Doughty; *Documents Relating to the Constitutional History of Canada, 1759–91*, edited by Shortt and Doughty; and the *Journals* of the House of Commons and the House of Lords. The most valuable source-books on general commerce were those by Adam Anderson and David McPherson. The most important contemporary works were: Bryan Edwards, *History Civil, and Commercial, of the British Colonies in the West Indies*, and Lord Sheffield, *Observations on the Commerce of the American States.* Both were mainly propagandist writings, and the contemporary influence of the latter was particularly great. Both contain stores of statistical data, but where these have been used, I have endeavoured to check them with the figures of the Board of Trade.

MANUSCRIPT SOURCES

I. MSS. OF THE PUBLIC RECORD OFFICE OF GREAT BRITAIN

A. Colonial Office Papers

1. *Canada. Original Correspondence, Board of Trade.*

C.O. 5/2 contains important reports on the Quebec and West Indian trade, 1777–1807.

Original Correspondence, Secretary of State.

C.O. 5/8. Despatches and Miscellany, 1780–83.

C.O. 5/25. Orders in Council sent to Board of Trade, February 1st, 1768, to December 16th, 1768 (fol. 69); petition for grant of minerals and metals around Lake Superior; also

C.O. 5/27. Folios 255 and 257.

C.O. 5/30–2. Instructions to the Board of Trade (Orders in Council, 1775–94).

C.O. 5/43. Miscellaneous Correspondence. Papers 4, 13, 17 and 21 contain papers on Canada's situation in 1763.

C.O. 5/61–187. Correspondence of the Secretary of State, of varying importance. 153 contains a letter from Germaine to the Lords of Treasury, and 154, letters of Maurice Morgan and William Eden on English manufactures.

C.O. 5/216–70. Entry Books of Letters, Instructions, Commissions, Warrants, etc.

C.O. 42/1–12. Original Correspondence, Board of Trade, Quebec, consisting mainly of reports.

C.O. 42/13–84. Original Correspondence—to the Secretary of State from Quebec. The important volumes are 14–21, 24–51, 58–73, 82–3.

C.O. 42/87–8. These volumes contain " Promiscuous Papers " for the period, 1762–89.

C.O. 43/1–16. Entry Books of Commissions, Instructions, Letters, Warrants, etc., to Quebec. The important volumes are 2–10, 13–15. Nos. 3 and 4 are Commissions ; 5, 6 and 7 are Entry Books.

C.O. 44. Containing the substance of " Acts " passed in connection with Quebec.

C.O. 45/1–13. Sessional Papers—Minutes of the Quebec Council, 1764–91.

C.O. 47/110. Advocate-General Marriott's Code of Law for the Province of Quebec.

C.O. 47/111. Court of Common Pleas Appeal—Taylor v. Rex, *re* the costs of Indian supply.

C.O. 47/112. Observations, Political and Commercial, on Canada, 1778.

2. *Jamaica. Original Correspondence, Board of Trade.*

C.O. 137/71, 72 and 79. Regarding the scarcity of provisions, as a result of hurricanes, earthquakes, tidal waves, fever.

C.O. 137/84–5. Regarding the closing of the ports to Americans.

C.O. 137/87 (1787–89). Contains a report of the legislative Committee on the state of the rum and molasses trade between the West Indies and British North America ; also shipping returns.

C.O. 137/92 (1793–94). Reveals the continued shortage of lumber and the need for opening the island's ports.

3. *Nova Scotia and Cape Breton.*

C.O. 217/43–53. Governor's Correspondence.

C.O. 323/34. (Official Correspondence, Secretary of State.) Law Officers' reports on Colonial Acts.

C.O. 388/59 and C.O. 390/9. Board of Trade Commercial, 1725–71. *Index*, *8367–74*, provides a general index to this correspondence.

B. Board of Trade, Original Correspondence.

B.T. 5/1. West Indies and American Trade.

B.T. 5/2. June, 1784–January, 1786, Intercourse between Quebec, U.S., N.B. and N.S., folios 203, 205, 242.

B.T. 5/4. Inland Trade with Canada, fol. 336.

B.T. 5/6. January–December, 1790. (P. 11, U.S. and Quebec Trade; fol. 179, Allen and Vermont.)

B.T. 6/85–6. American Intercourse with Great Britain, 1783–6.

B.T. 6/87. *Ibid.*, with N.S. and Newfoundland.

B.T. 6/96. Navigation Laws.

B.T. 6/97–9. Hemp and Flax only.

B.T. 6/102. Nova Scotia and Quebec.

C. Treasury.

Treas. 1/465. Letter from F. Mackay to Treasury, *re* survey of part of Lake Champlain and trees for Navy, Montreal, May 15th, 1776.

Treas. 1/525. F. 177; Petition of John Shoolbred, merchant in trade to Canada, 1776.

Treas. 4/12. Petition *re* fishing trade from settlers in Quebec and U.S., April 7th, 1773.

Minute Books.

Treas. 29/47. February–November, 1778, Affairs of Florida, ceded isles, Canada and N.S.

Imports from Canada. (*Provisions, Trade*).

Treas. 64/72. Vessels from Britain, British American Colonies and West Indies from U.S. with produce of U.S. (*Tables*).

Treas. 64/115. In-letters from Commander-in-Chief in Canada, 1778–81.

D. War Office.

W.O. 1/11. Letters from Generals Carleton and Haldimand, almost entirely military despatches, 1776–81.

E. Chatham Papers, in Public Record Office.

First Series, 1–100.

Second Series, 101–363.

Bundle 79. Admiralty Papers relating to Canada. State of exports from Great Britain to North America, 1764. Fisheries of North America. Bounties.

Bundle 98. Papers relating to Canada.

Bundle 343. Papers relating to North America. Observations on American Treaty, retention of posts, 1782–84.

Bundle 344. Considerations on abandoning posts, an unsigned and undated letter.

Bundles 346, 351 and 352. Papers relating to West Indies.

F. Privy Council Records.

P.C. 1/16. Non-Colonial A. A. 10, 1784, Bundle of about 28 papers, *re* bounties on Hemp and Flax.

P.C. 1/16. Colonial. B. B. Addenda to earlier list, printed.

II. CANADIAN ARCHIVES AT OTTAWA

Calendar of Shelburne Correspondence, calendared in the report of the Public Archives of Canada for 1912 and 1921, Vol. 66, Imports and bounties, 1766, 1770, 1776–80; Vol. 71, on peace of 1783; Vol. 72, Canadian merchants to Shelburne; Vol. 88, Canada and Cuba; Vol. 111, Canadian Exports; Vols. 138 and 144, navy and timber. (Transcripts with Stevens and Brown, 4, Trafalgar Square, London.) The Shelburne MSS. are now in the William L. Clements' Library at the University of Michigan, Ann Arbor. See *Bulletin of the Institute of Historical Research*, Vol. I, No. 3, pp. 77–80, Feb., 1924, where Professor Clarence W. Alvord has described this collection.

Calendar of Haldimand Collection; reports of Canadian Archives for 1886, 1887, 1888, transcribed at Ottawa under B. 175. The Report for 1890 contains a valuable note—" Relations with the United States after the Peace of 1783 " (Canadian Archives Q., 27–1, p. 38).

Correspondence Politique Etats Unis, beginning 1774, Vols. 1–25, No. 63, Luzerne to (Vergennes) No. 240, May 21st, 1782; Vol. 22; "Mémoires sur la situation du Commerce Américain et les moyens de le retablir." (Transcripts with Stevens and Brown, 4, Trafalgar Square, London.)

III. MSS. OF THE BRITISH MUSEUM.

Additional MS., 8133B. Folios 141, Board of Trade on hemp; 177–9, Naval Stores; 194–5, Rum; 280, Spruce from Canada.

Additional MS., 8133C. Folio 149, Bounties (Nov. 6th, 1781).

Additional MSS., 14034–5. Papers and Maps on West Indies and Canada. Folio 221 on Quebec. Collection of papers of Board of Trade relating to West Indies, America, Africa and Canaries, etc. (N.B. George Chalmers' reports.)

Additional MS., 18274. *Ed. Long's Observations on the West Indies Trade*, 1784.

Additional MS., 21759. Letters *re* upper Posts, 1778–82.

Additional MS., 21835. Haldimand Collection, Correspondence relating to Vermont.

Additional MSS., 21858–9. Papers and Accounts, Rec. General's Department.

Additional MS., 21861. *Haldimand Papers* relative to Public Service in Canada.

Additional MS., 21861. Trade, 1768–83. Miscellany.

Additional MS., 21880. Miscellaneous.

Additional MS., 21882. Miscellaneous.

Additional MS., 21885. Miscellaneous.

Additional MSS., 24131–3. Shelburne Extracts. Abstracts of English State Letters and official papers.

Additional MS., 24323. Correspondence of Sir William, Guy and John Johnson, to John Blackburn, merchant of London.

Additional MS., 26052. *Marriott's Report on Canada*, 1771.

Additional MSS., 34412–18. Correspondence of Lord Auckland (Wm. Eden).

Additional MS., 34415. Folio 568, *On State of the Nation*, Dean of Gloucester, 1777.

Additional MS., 34461. Folio 332, Memo. of goods shipped to Canada, 1778.

Additional MSS., 35374–5. Letters from John Yorke to Lord Hardwicke, 1747–87. (Yorke was Commissioner of Board of Trade and Lord of Admiralty.)

Additional MS., 38346. Folio 359, Observations on Commerce and Shipbuilding in 1786.

Additional MS., 38348. Folio 82, Objections to altering duties on rum distillation, 1787. Folios 58, 112, 113, Tables of exports and imports (much over-valued).

Additional MS., 38350. Folio 31; notes, errors in trade schedule, *re* (Act 28, Geo. III, c. 39) W.I. and Canadian free trade agreement (1790).

Additional MS., 38388. Folios 9–139, *passim*, Minutes of Committee of Trade regarding Lumber.

Additional MS., 38389. *Minutes of Committee of Trade*, 1785–91. Folios 20, 79b, 90b, 183b, 259.

Additional MS., 38390. Folios 52b, 109b, 150, 169b, 170b, 175–6.

Additional MS., 38391. Folios 21, 35b, Report of Quebec Legislative Council on Hemp culture, January 29th, 1787; for rum trade, March 31st, 1788, see folios 47b; 1–153b, *passim*.

Additional MS., 38392. Folios 1–166b, *passim*.

Additional MS., 38393. Folios 84b, 157, 157b.

Additional MS., 38394. Folios 3, 6b, 11.

Kings MS., 213. Folio 59, Memo. of officer on Canada, 1765.

PRINTED SOURCES

A. Collections, Journals, Publications of Documents, Personal Correspondence, Etc.

Acts of the Privy Council, Colonial Series (Grant and Munro, ed.), Hereford, 1908–11.

Albemarle, Lord (ed.). *Memoirs of Lord Rockingham*, 2 vols. London, 1852.

Bedford Correspondence, 3 vols. Selected from originals at Woburn Abbey; introduction by Fred J. Russell. London, 1842–6.

Canadian Archives, *Reports* on, for 1888, 1890, 1904, 1912 and 1921. Ed. D. Brymner and later, Arthur G. Doughty, Ottawa.

Cavendish, Sir Henry. *Debates of the House of Commons during the Parliament of 1768*, 2 vols. (May, 1768–March, 1771). London, 1841.

Donne, W. B. (ed.). *Correspondence between George III and Lord North*, 2 vols. London, 1867.

Dropmore Papers. Official MSS. of J. B. Fortescue preserved at Dropmore, 10 volumes, in Historical Manuscripts Commission Publications—containing the private papers of Lord Grenville, British Secretary of State for Home Affairs, 1789–91. London, 1894, etc.

Fortescue, Hon. Sir John William. *Correspondence of King George III from 1760 to December, 1783;* printed from the original papers in the Royal Archives at Windsor Castle, 6 vols. London, 1927–28.

Gentleman's Magazine and Historical Chronicle, by Sylvanus Urban, Gent. London, 1824.

Hamilton, Sir R. V. (ed.). *Letters and Papers of Admiral of the Fleet, Sir Thomas Byam Martin*, 3 vols. London, 1901.

Kimball, Gertrude Selwyn (ed.). *Correspondence of William Pitt when Secretary of State*, with colonial governors and military and naval commissioners in America, 2 vols. New York, 1906.

Knox MS. in Historical MSS. Commission Report (Various Collections, Vol. VI). London, 1909.

Laprade, W. T. (ed.). *Parliamentary Papers of John Robinson, 1774–84*. London, 1922.

Laughton, Sir John Knox (ed.). *Letters and Papers of Charles Lord Barham*, 2 vols. London, 1910.

Lincoln, C. H. (ed.). *Correspondence of William Shirley*, Governor of Massachusetts and Military Commander in America, 1731–60, National Society of Colonial Dames of America. New York, 1912.

The Parliamentary History of England, 1066–1803, ed. Cobbett and Wright, 36 vols.

The Parliamentary Register (1743–1802), 88 vols. Compiled from newspapers and magazines—and supplements many gaps in Cobbett.

Russell, Lord John (ed.). *Memorials and Correspondence of Charles James Fox*, 2 vols. London, 1853.

Shortt and Doughty. *Documents relating to the Constitutional History of Canada*, 1759–91. Canadian Archives, Ottawa, 1918.

Smith, William J. (ed.). *Grenville Papers*, being the correspondence of Richard Grenville, Earl Temple and George Grenville, and friends and contemporaries, 4 vols. London, 1853.

The Statutes at Large of England—from Magna Charta to (32–3 Vict.) By O. Ruffhead, etc., 52 vols. London, 1769–1862.

Stopford-Sackville MSS. in Historical Manuscripts Commission Publications, 2 vols. London, 1904 and 1910.

Taylor, W. S. and Pringle, J. H. (ed.). *Correspondence of William Pitt, Earl of Chatham*, 4 vols. London, 1838–40.

Turner, F. J. *Correspondence of the French Ministers to the United States, 1791–7*. American Hist. Assoc. Annual Reports, 1903.

Wharton, Francis. *Diplomatic Correspondence of the American Revolution*. Washington, 1889.

Wright, J. (ed.). *Speeches of the Rt. Hon. Charles James Fox in the House of Commons*, 6 vols. London, 1815.

Newspapers—

London Chronicle, years 1774–91, Cambridge University Library.

Guides—

Andrews, Charles M. (and Davenport, Frances G.). *Guide to the Manuscript Materials for the History of the United States to 1783*, in the British Museum, in Minor London Archives, and in the Libraries of Oxford and Cambridge. Carnegie Institution, Washington, 1908.

Andrews, Charles M. *Guide to the Materials for American History to 1783*, in the Public Record Office of Great Britain. Vol. I, *State Papers*. Vol. II, *Departmental and Miscellaneous Papers*. Carnegie Institution, Washington, 1912.

Bell, Herbert C. and Parker, David W. *Guide to British West Indian Archive Materials in London and in the Islands for the History of the United States*. Washington, D.C., published by the Carnegie Institution of Washington, 1926.

Historical Publications relating to Canada (University of Toronto), edited by G. M. Wrong. A bibliography of modern writers on Canada. Continued in *Canadian Historical Review.*

Paxson, Frederick L. and Paullin, Chas. O. *Guide to the Materials for the History of the U.S. since 1783 in London Archives.* Carnegie Institution, Washington, 1914.

Ragatz, L. J. *A Guide to the Official Correspondence of the Governors of the British West India Colonies with the Secretary of State, 1763–1833.* London, 1923.

B. Contemporary Historical Works and Memoirs.

Anderson, David. *Canada, or a view of the importance of the British American Colonies.* London, 1814.

The Annual Register, or a view of the history, politics and literature, for the years 1758–76 (London, 1789).

Brougham (Henry), 1st Baron. *An Enquiry into the Colonial Policy of the European Powers,* 2 vols. Edinburgh, 1803.

Burke, Edmund. (1) *A Short Account of the late Short Administration.* John Almon, London, 1787.

(2) *An Account of the European Settlements in America,* 6th ed., 2 vols. London, 1777.

(3) *Thoughts on the Cause of the Present Discontents,* 1770.

(4) *Speech on American Taxation,* 1774.

(5) *Speech on Moving the Resolutions for Conciliation with the Colonies, March,* 1775.

Chalmers, George. *An estimate of the comparative strength of Britain during the present and four preceding reigns . . . to which is added an essay on population by Chief Justice Hale.* London, 1782.

Edwards, Bryan. *History, Civil and Commercial, of British Colonies in the West Indies.* London, 1807.

Hutchinson, Thomas. *Diary and Letters,* ed. Peter Orlando Hutchinson. London, 1883.

Hume, David. *Three Essays*—I, On the Balance of Trade ; II, On the Jealousy of Trade ; III, On the Balance of Power. London, 1787.

Huskisson, William. *Edinburgh Review,* August, 1825, vol. 42, containing the substance of two speeches delivered in the House of Commons on the 21st and 25th March, 1825, on *The Colonial Policy and Foreign Commerce of the Country.*

Kippis, Andrew. *Considerations on the Provisional Treaty with America,* and the preliminary articles of peace with France and Spain. A defence of the Treaty of 1783. London, 1783.

Knox, William. *Extra-Official State Papers.* London, 1789.

Oldfield, T. H. B. *Representative History of Great Britain and Ireland,* 6 vols. London, 1816.

Pownall, Thomas. *Two Memorials,* not originally intended for publication; now published, with an explanatory preface by Governor Pownall. London, 1782.

The Administration of the Colonies, 4th edition. London, 1767.

Raynal (Guillaume, T. F.), Abbé. *A Philosophical and Political History of the Settlements and Trade of the Europeans in the East and West Indies,* 2nd ed., 6 vols. London, 1783.

Rose, George A. *Brief Examination into the Increase of the Revenue, Commerce and Navigation of Great Britain since the Conclusion of the Peace in 1783.* London, 1792 (2nd ed., 1799).

Sheffield, Lord. *Observations on the Commerce of the American States* (with an appendix), 2nd edition. London, 1783.

Smith, Adam. *The Wealth of Nations,* ed. E. Cannan, 3rd edition. London, 1922.

Tucker, Josiah. (Tract V) *The Respective Pleas and Arguments of the Mother Country and of the Colonies distinctly set forth,* etc. Gloucester, 1775.

An Humble Address and Earnest Appeal to those respectable personages in Great Britain and Ireland who . . . are the ablest to judge and the fittest to decide, whether a connection with, or a separation from the Continental Colonies of America be most for the national advantage, etc. Gloucester, 1775.

A Series of Answers to certain popular objections against separating from the Rebellious Colonies and discarding them entirely. Gloucester, 1776.

A Brief Essay on the advantages and disadvantages which respectively attend France and Great Britain with regard to trade. London, 1787.

Four Letters on Important National Subjects addressed to the Earl of Shelburne. Gloucester, 1783.

Walpole, Horace. *Letters* (ed. Toynbee). Oxford, 1903.

Wraxall, Nathaniel. *Historical Memoirs,* 4 vols. London, 1818.

Wraxall, Nathaniel. *A Short Review of the Political State of Great Britain at the commencement of the year 1787.* London, 1787.

Young, Arthur. *Travels in France,* during the years 1787, 1788, 1789 (Miss Betham Edwards' edition). London, 1905.

C. General Sources on Commerce.

Anderson, Adam. *Historical and Chronological Deduction of the Origin of Commerce*, 4 vols. London, 1787–9.

Beawes, Wyndham. *Lex Mercatoria*, 5th edition. London, 1792.

Burnet, E. C. *London Merchants on American Trade, 1783.* A.H.R., Vol. XVIII, p. 769.

Macpherson, David. *Annals of Commerce, Manufactures, Fisheries and Navigation*, 4 vols. London, 1805.

McCulloch, J. R. *Dictionary of Commerce and Commercial Navigation*, etc. London, 1832–9. Latest edition with a supplement, by A. J. Wilson. London, 1882.

D. Pamphlets.

Advantageous Situation of Great Britain on the Reduction of America. London, 1777.

The Colonial Policy of Great Britain considered with Relation to her North American Provinces and West Indian Possessions, by a British Traveller, Anon. London, 1816.

Considerations on the Policy, Commerce and Circumstances of the Kingdom. London, 1771.

Essay on Trade and Commerce containing Observations on Taxes etc., together with some interesting reflections on the Importance of our Trade to America. London, 1770.

Essays—Commercial and Political—on the Real and Relative Interests of Imperial and Dependent States, 1777.

Essay on the True Interests and Resources of the Empire of Great Britain and Ireland, etc., by the Earl of A——l. Dublin, 1783.

Letter, to the Earl of Shelburne on the peace. Sgnd. Portius, Feb. 5, 1783. London, 1783.

Macpherson, Jas. The Rights of Great Britain asserted against the claims of America, being an answer to the Declaration of the General Congress, 3rd ed. Dublin, 1776.

Present State of Great Britain and North America with regard to Agriculture (1767), by Samuel Lalham Mitchell.

Reflections on the Preliminary and Provisional Articles. London, 1783.

The State of the Nation in 1777, compared with the State of the Nation in the famous year of Conquest and of Glory, 1759, by the Dean of Gloucester.

Unanimity in all parts of the British Commonwealth necessary to its preservation, interest and happiness, etc. London, 1778.

MONOGRAPHS AND SPECIAL WORKS

Albion, Robert Greenhalgh. *Forests and Sea Power.* Harvard Economic Series, Vol. XXIX. Cambridge, U.S.A., 1926.

Alvord, C. W. *The Mississippi Valley in British Politics.* A Study of Trade, Land Speculation and Experiments in Imperialism, culminating in the American Revolution (2 vols.). Cleveland, 1917.

Basye, A. H. *The Lords Commissioners of Trade and Plantations (commonly known as the Board of Trade)*, 1748–82. New Haven, London, 1925.

Basye, A. H. The Secretary of State for the Colonies, 1768–82. *A.H.R.*, Vol. 28, 1922.

Beer, G. L. *British Colonial Policy, 1754–65.* New York, 1907.

Beer, G. L. *Commercial Policy of England towards the American Colonies.* New York, 1893.

Bell, H. C. British Commercial Policy in the West Indies, 1785–93. *E.H.R.*, July, 1916.

Bemis, Samuel Flagg. *Jay's Treaty, 1794. A Study in Commerce and Diplomacy.* Knights of Columbus Hist. Series. New York, 1923.

Bemis, S. F. " Jay's Treaty and the North-West Boundary Gap." *A.H.R.*, Vol. XXVII, 465.

Bourinot, J. (1) *Canada under British Rule, 1760–1900.* Cambridge Historical Series, Cambridge, 1900.

Bowden, Witt. The Influence of the Manufacturers on some of the Early Policies of William Pitt. *A.H.R.*, Vol. XXIX, July, 1924.

Bowley, A. L. *England's Foreign Trade.* London, 1897.

Brown, George W. The St. Lawrence in the Boundary Settlement of 1783. *C.H.R.*, September, 1928.

Burt, A. L. (and Bradley, A. G.). *Sir Guy Carleton. Lord Dorchester.* (Makers of Canada Series.) Vol. III. London and Toronto, 1926.

Cambridge History of British Foreign Policy, 1783–1919. Ed. by Sir A. W. Ward and G. P. Gooch. Cambridge, 1922.

Canada and its Provinces, a History of the Canadian People and their Institutions. Shortt and Doughty, general editors. Edinburgh Edition, Toronto, 1914.

Clapham, J. H. The Last Years of the Navigation Acts. *E.H.R.*, Vol. XXV.

Clapham, J. H. *An Economic History of Modern Britain*, Vol. I. Cambridge, 1926.

Clarke, Mary P. The Board of Trade at Work. *A.H.R.*, Vol. XVII.

Clowes, Sir. W. Laird. *The Royal Navy, a History from the Earliest Times to the Present,* Vol. IV, Chap. xxxi. London, 1899.

Coffin, V. *The Province of Quebec and the American Revolution.* Bulletin of the University of Wisconsin, Madison, 1896.

Corwin, Edward S. *French Policy and the American Alliance of 1778.* Princeton University Press, Princeton, 1916.

Coupland, R. *The Quebec Act. A Study in Statesmanship.* Clarendon Press, Oxford, 1925.

Cunningham, William. *The Growth of English Industry and Commerce.* 3rd ed., Cambridge, 1896.

Davidson, G. C. *The North-West Company.* University of California Hist. Studies, Berkeley, 1918.

Davidson, John. *Commercial Federation and Colonial Trade Policy.* London, 1900.

Doniol, H. Le Ministère des Affaires étrangères de France sous le Compte de Vergennes. *Revue d'Histoire Diplomatique.* Vol. VII. Paris, 1893.

Fitzmaurice, Lord. *Life of the Earl of Shelburne, afterwards First Marquess of Lansdowne,* 2 vols. Second and revised edition. London, 1912.

Galpin, William Freeman. *The Grain Supply of England during the Napoleonic Period.* Michigan University History and Political Studies. New York, 1925.

Grant, W. L. *Canada or Guadaloupe? A.H.R.*, July, 1912, Vol. XVII, p. 740.

Green, Walford Davis. *William Pitt, Earl of Chatham, and the Growth and Division of the British Empire.* New York, 1901.

Haliburton, Thomas Chandler. *Bubbles of Canada.* London, 1839.

Hertz (now Hurst), G. B. *The Old Colonial System.* University of Manchester Publications. Historical Series, No. 3. Manchester, 1905.

Hotblack, Kate. *Chatham's Colonial Policy.* A Study in the fiscal and economical implications of the Colonial Policy of the Elder Pitt. New York and London, 1917.

Hunt, W. *Political History of England,* Vol. X, 1760–1801. London, 1924.

Johnson, W. F. *America's Foreign Relations,* 2 vols. New York, 1921.

Kapp, Friedrich. *Leben des Amerikanischen Generals, Johann Kalb.* Stuttgart, 1862.

Kennedy, W. P. M. *Documents of the Canadian Constitution, 1759–1915.* Toronto, 1918.

Kennedy. W. P. M. *The Constitution of Canada.* Oxford, 1922.

Kingsford, William. *History of Canada*, 10 vols., Vols. V. and VI. London, 1892.

Knowles, Lillian. *The Economic Development of the Overseas Empire, 1763–1914*, 2 vols. London, 1924, 1930.

Lecky, William E. Hartpole. *History of England in the Eighteenth Century*, Vols. I–VII, new edition. London, 1892.

Lewis, George Cornwall. *Essay on Government of Dependencies*. Introd. by C. P. Lucas. Clarendon Press, Oxford, 1891.

Lewis, George Cornwall. *Essays on Administrations of Great Britain, 1783–1830*. Ed. Sir E. Head. London, 1864.

Lower, A. R. M. The Forest in New France. Can. Historical Association Report, 1928, pp. 78–90.

Lingelbach, A. N. The Inception of the British Board of Trade. *A.H.R.*, July, 1925

Lucas, Reginald. *Lord North, 1732–92*, 2 vols. London, 1913.

McIlwraith, Jean. *Life of General Haldimand*. (Makers of Canada Series.) London, Toronto, 1926.

McLaughlin, A. C. Western Posts and British Debts. Annual Reports, American Historical Assoc., pp. 412–14, 1894.

Martin, Chester. *Empire and Commonwealth. Studies in Governance and Self-Government in Canada*. Oxford, 1929.

Morgan, W. T. English Fear of " Encirclement " in the Seventeenth Century. *C.H.R.*, March, 1929.

Munro, W. B. *The Seigneurial System in Canada*. A Study in French Colonial Policy. Harvard University Press, Cambridge, Mass., 1907.

Munro, W. B. *The Seigneurs of Old Canada. Chronicles of Canada*. Toronto, 1920.

Munro, W. B. *Documents Relating to the Seigneurial Tenure in Canada*. Champlain Society Publications. Toronto, 1908.

Namier, L. B. *Structure of Politics at the Accession of George III*. London, 1929.

Newman, Bertram. *Edmund Burke*. London, 1927.

Nicholson, J. Shield. *A Project of Empire*. A critical study of the Economics of Imperialism, with special reference to the ideas of Adam Smith. London, 1909.

Penson, L. M. The London West India Interest in the Eighteenth Century. *E.H.R.*, October, 1921.

Penson, L. M. *Colonial Agents of the British West Indies*. A study in colonial administration mainly in the eighteenth century. London, 1924.

Perkins, James Breck. *France in the American Revolution*. London, 1911.

Pitman, F. W. *Development of British West Indies, 1700–63.* Yale Historical Publications, New Haven, 1917.

Porritt, E. and A. G. *The Unreformed House of Commons*, 2 vols. Cambridge, 1903.

Roscher, Wilhelm. *Kolonien, Kolonialpolitik and Auswanderung.* Leipzig, 1885.

Schlesinger, Arthur Meier. *Colonial Merchants and the American Revolution.* (Columbia University Studies in History, Economics, etc.) New York, 1917.

Schmoller, Gustav. *The Mercantile System.* Ashley's Economic Classics, London, 1896.

Smith, Sir Hubert Llewellyn. *The Board of Trade.* London, 1928.

Stanhope, Philip Henry (5th Earl). *Life of Pitt*, 3 vols. Vol I, London, 1879.

Stevens, W. E. *The North-West Fur Trade, 1763–1800.* (Univ. of Illinois Studies in the Social Sciences, Vol. XIV, No. 3, Sept., 1926.) University of Illinois, Urbana, 1926.

Stuart, Dorothy Margaret. *Horace Walpole.* English Men of Letters, ed. by J. C. Squire. London, 1927.

Temperley, H. W. V. Chatham, North and America. *Quarterly Review*, October, 1914. No. 441.

Thackeray, Francis. *Life of Chatham*, 2 vols. London, 1827.

Trevelyan, G. O. (Sir). *The American Revolution II*, pt. ii. London, 1905.

Troup, Sir Chas. Ed. *The Secretary of State, Home Office.* (Whitehall Series.) London, 1925.

Turner, F. J. Policy of France toward the Mississippi Valley in the Period of Washington and Adams. *A.H.R.*, Vol. X. January, 1905.

Turner, F. J. English Policy towards America, 1790–91. *A.H.R.*, Vols. VII and VIII.

Van Tyne, C. H. *The American Revolution, 1776–83.* New York and London, 1918.

Van Tyne, C. H. *The Loyalists in the American Revolution.* New York, 1922.

Van Tyne, C. H. *The Causes of the War of Independence.* Being the first volume of a History of the Founding of the American Republic. London and Cambridge, Mass., 1921.

Veitch, George Stead. *The Genesis of Parliamentary Reform*, with an introduction by Ramsay Muir. London, 1913.

Wallace, W. Stewart. *The Maseres Letters, 1766–68*, edited with Introduction, Notes and Appendices. University of Toronto Studies in History and Economics. Toronto, 1919.

Wallace, W. Stewart. *The United Empire Loyalists.* Toronto, 1920.

Wallace, W. S. The Beginnings of British Rule in Canada. *C.H.R.*, September, 1925, No. 3.

Williams, Basil. *Life of Pitt, Earl of Chatham*, 2 vols. London, 1913.

INDEX